Also fro

You can develop the skills to meet the needs of learners in any learning environment.

This approachable, in-depth guide unites the adaptability of Universal Design for Learning with the flexibility of blended learning, equipping educators with the tools they need to create relevant, authentic, and meaningful learning pathways to meet students where they're at, no matter the time and place or their pace and path. With step-by-step guidance and clear strategies, authors Katie Novak and Catlin Tucker empower teachers to implement these frameworks in the classroom, with a focus on cultivating community, building equity, and increasing accessibility for all learners.

As we face increasing uncertainty and frequent disruption to traditional ways of living and learning, *UDL and Blended Learning* offers bold, innovative, inclusive solutions for navigating a range of learning landscapes, from the home to the classroom and all points in between, no matter what obstacles may lie ahead.

Catlin Tucker and Katie Novak have worked with too many educators who are frustrated and disillusioned with the teaching profession. They know that teachers are drowning in work and unrealistic demands. Many are mentally and emotionally exhausted by the uncertainty and constant change created by the pandemic. In this follow-up to *UDL and Blended Learning*, the authors have set out to help teachers reimagine their approach to this work so that it is sustainable and rewarding.

Each chapter in *The Shift to Student-Led* takes apart one traditional teacher-led workflow, examining the problems it presents teachers and students, what the research says versus what the reality in the classroom is, and how UDL and blended learning can free teachers from the "sage on the stage" role and place students at the center of their learning. These reimagined student-led workflows help students develop self-awareness, internal motivation, and self-regulation skills, which are critical to becoming expert learners.

Intended for K–12 educators, instructional coaches, and school leaders who want to create academically robust, inclusive learning communities, this book is full of principles, strategies, and resources that can be put into practice right away and at any level.

This book is an essential resource for all educators. To address declining literacy skills, every educator needs to become a teacher of writing. In every grade and subject, the writing process enables students to interpret complex ideas, cultivate their individual voices, and shape and share their learning.

As writing becomes more efficient with the aid of AI chatbots, there's an unparalleled opportunity for educators across all content areas to reimagine their approach to writing. In *Shift Writing into the Classroom*, UDL and blended learning experts Catlin R. Tucker and Katie Novak invite educators to focus on human connection, sitting alongside learners to understand their specific needs and provide individualized instruction and support across *all* grades and content areas. Tucker and Novak transform traditional writing workflows to provide students with meaningful opportunities in the classroom to work through the writing process, collaborate with peers, and produce original writing that addresses task, purpose, and audience creatively and authentically.

Ideal for schools and districts prioritizing the integration of literacy across the curriculum, this book offers practical guidance, strategies, and resources to elevate students' writing abilities in every subject.

Elevating Educational Design with AI

ELEVATING
Educational Design with AI

MAKING LEARNING ACCESSIBLE,
INCLUSIVE, AND EQUITABLE

CATLIN R. TUCKER & **KATIE NOVAK**

Elevating Educational Design with AI: Making Learning Accessible, Inclusive, and Equitable
© 2025 Catlin R. Tucker and Katie Novak

Published by IMPress, a division of Dave Burgess Consulting, Inc.
IMPressbooks.org
DaveBurgessConsulting.com

Paperback ISBN: 978-1-948334-77-8
Ebook ISBN: 978-1-948334-78-5

Cover and interior design by Liz Schreiter
Edited and produced by Reading List Editorial
ReadingListEditorial.com

To all the brilliant educators out there—don't fear the robots! Together, we can use AI to level up, but the heart of teaching will always be human.

Contents

PART I: ESTABLISHING A FOUNDATION

PART II: DESIGNING FOR EQUITY

PART III: PERSONALIZING LEARNING

PART IV: BUILDING RESILIENCE

Tables, Figures, and Planning Templates

INTRODUCTION

AI as a Catalyst for Equitable, Student-Centered Learning

50 Edtech Tools in 50 Minutes

Catlin   In 2013, my good friend Alice Keeler informed me (Alice doesn't ask!) that I was going with her to my first International Society for Technology in Education (ISTE) conference.

At that point, I was a mom with two young kids who was also teaching full time, and I had no idea how I would financially or logistically swing a trip to San Antonio, Texas, for three days to attend the conference. Thankfully, I submitted a conference proposal to facilitate two half-day workshops to cover the cost of my flight, and Alice invited me to share a hotel room. Once all the details were in place, I felt giddy; I was excited to learn more about leveraging technology to enhance my lessons and engage my students in meaningful learning.

I'll never forget walking through the halls of ISTE, crowded with educators searching for the sessions in a maze of hallways and buildings. As I walked to the location for a session I wanted to attend, my curiosity was piqued by a room with people spilling out of it. Assuming the mass of people trying to enter was a sign that the session would be worthwhile, I abandoned my initial plan and decided to check it out.

I wedged my way into the room, past other teachers standing in the doorway, all of whom were clearly eyeing the prospect of finding a seat for the hour-long session. As I nestled into an available opening against the wall, I caught sight of the presenters' screen: two women were going to present "50 Edtech Tools in 50 Minutes." I remember thinking, *OK, cool. I'll get some EdTech tools I can add to my technology toolbox!*

Over the course of the next fifty minutes, the presenters reviewed one technology tool approximately every minute. They introduced each tool, providing a brief introduction to its functionality and the grade levels the tool was appropriate for. I jotted down as much as possible, but it was a blur of information, and I left the session a little dazed from the array of EdTech tools available to us as educators.

While the premise of the session was catchy, I can't say that it ultimately made much of a difference to my teaching or my students. Instead, when I think back to the conference sessions that significantly impacted my teaching, I find that I learned the most from the ones that integrated technology with pedagogy, demonstrating how technology could be used to activate lesson engagement, give students agency over aspects of their learning experience, or streamline my workflows to better meet the needs of all students. Ultimately, it was much more valuable when technology tools were paired with strong pedagogical practices; this combination empowered me to confidently leverage technology to enhance my teaching practice and improve the quality of my students' learning experience.

I'm having flashbacks to "50 EdTech Tools in 50 Minutes" in the wake of AI's explosion onto the educational scene. Every day on Instagram, I see teachers sharing AI-powered tools and explaining the features and functionality. They demonstrate the efficiency and simplicity with which these tools generate lists of depth of knowledge (DoK) questions, create quick assessments, and spit out lessons or entire units. I can understand and appreciate the excitement about these tools since lesson planning is a time-consuming endeavor. However, there's a piece of the conversation and, ultimately, the design puzzle missing for me: we need to understand how educators can use AI tools to architect student-centered learning experiences that *better* meet the needs of *all* learners.

Educators' understanding of their students is essential to designing effective and equitable learning experiences. When educators simply copy and paste a standard into an AI-powered education tool to generate a lesson or learning activity, they risk losing the personal touch and critical thinking that are crucial to effective teaching. These tools can provide a starting point, but they often lack the depth and customization needed to address the unique strengths, needs, and interests of individual students. The nuanced understanding of classroom dynamics, student backgrounds, and learning preferences that educators bring to their practice is irreplaceable.

Relying heavily on AI-generated lessons can also perpetuate the use of the one-size-fits-all learning experience, undermining efforts to create inclusive and differentiated learning environments where all students can thrive. AI tools cannot account for the varied pace at which students learn or the diverse ways they engage with material. Educators must take the time to review, adapt, and supplement AI-generated lessons to ensure they are culturally responsive, engaging, and tailored to their students.

If we're going to take AI seriously as a tool for transforming education, then we need to ensure we're using it to its greatest potential. We can continue to use AI-powered education tools to churn out one-size-fits-few lessons, activities, and assessments. Or we can use them to design with a higher level of intentionality in a fraction of the time. As I consider the future of education, I don't want AI to become a free version of Teachers Pay Teachers, where we grab a lesson created by someone (or in the case of AI, some*thing*) else and then simply deploy that lesson in a one-size-fits-all fashion, without our unique class of students in mind. To make the most of AI, let's elevate the conversation beyond shiny novelty and focus on how we can use AI-powered tools in the service of strong pedagogical practices that offer equitable learning experiences for every student.

Why We Wrote This Book

We teach beautifully diverse groups of students with various skill levels, needs, language proficiencies, and learning preferences. This diversity should be seen as an asset to the learning environment, but our approach to lesson design and facilitation often makes it feel like a threat to effective teaching and learning because it cannot be served by the status quo—whole-group, teacher-led lessons. That diversity deserves more from the educational system.

Keyword Alert!

Universal Design for Learning (UDL): A comprehensive framework for the design of curriculums and learning environments, grounded in the belief that all students are capable of learning at high levels when designers embrace variability and eliminate barriers to learning with thoughtful design. UDL focuses on three core principles:

- Multiple means of engagement: using different methods to motivate and sustain students' interest in learning

- Multiple means of representation: providing diverse ways for students to perceive and comprehend information

- Multiple means of action and expression: offering various ways for students to demonstrate what they know.

The three principles of UDL empower educators to design lessons with firm goals and flexible means, ensuring that all learners, regardless of their variability, have opportunities to reflect on the goals and their strengths, preferences, and challenges. This approach fosters learner agency by enabling students to create personalized strategies that are relevant, authentic, and meaningful to their individual learning journeys.

Keyword Alert!

Understanding by design (UbD): The combination of active, engaged learning online with active, engaged learning offline to give students more control over the time, place, pace, and path of their learning. This blend of online and offline learning can happen in a traditional classroom, on a hybrid schedule, or in a remote learning course that has synchronous elements.

Before AI, designing for learner variability was an arduous process that may have felt unsustainable. One of the biggest hurdles we've encountered while facilitating workshops on blended learning models and Universal Design for Learning (UDL) is that educators do not have time to design student-centered learning experiences.

AI promises to simplify educator workload on several fronts, alleviating the pressure on teachers to spend hours designing lessons, providing feedback, and, in the not-too-distant future, accurately assessing student work. Yet if this vision for AI in EdTech is not implemented, educators may continue to face overwhelming work-loads, leading to burnout and decreased effectiveness in teaching. Additionally, students might miss out on the benefits of personalized learning experiences that AI can facilitate, potentially widening the achievement gap. We want AI to empower educators to design with a higher level of intentionality (not less).

While AI can significantly enhance educators' ability to address specific learning needs, to harness AI's potential in a way that truly benefits our students, we must first deeply understand our students' unique requirements and preferences. If we simply plug a standard or topic into an AI-powered tool to generate an activity, a set of depth of knowledge (DoK) questions, a vocabulary list, or an assessment, we save time. However, time saved doesn't necessarily change the quality of learning or improve the student experience.

While AI can be a powerful ally in streamlining educational tasks, the role of teachers remains crucial in validating and adapting

AI-generated outputs to meet the unique needs of our students. Ultimately, the synergy between AI efficiencies and human oversight ensures that technology enhances rather than diminishes the quality of education. In short, we don't want AI to replace the human element of education; we want AI to elevate it.

We don't want AI to replace the human element of education; we want AI to elevate it.

> **Keyword Alert!**
>
> **ChatGPT:** A large language model created by OpenAI. This AI can understand and generate text by predicting and creating relevant responses to different prompts. It is trained on a vast amount of text from various sources, helping it learn patterns, grammar, and context. ChatGPT was one of the first widely accessible models from OpenAI, making advanced AI text generation available to the public.

Our strategy for engaging with ChatGPT (or the AI chatbot of your choice!) involves using it as a collaborative partner in lesson design. By inputting specific standards or instructional goals, we can harness ChatGPT's ability to generate detailed lesson plans and activities that align with educational objectives.

To illustrate this, we began with a straightforward command: inserting a third-grade Common Core Math Standard into ChatGPT and requesting a lesson or sequence of lessons to teach that standard. Our goal was to explore how ChatGPT could help create a foundation for lesson planning while leaving room for our own customization and adaptation. By guiding ChatGPT with specific prompts and refining its outputs, we were able to produce high-quality, student-centered lesson plans that can be tailored to meet the diverse needs of our learners. Check out our process!

Catlin and Katie: Can you write a lesson plan to teach the following third-grade math standard? "Use multiplication and division within 100 to solve word problems in situations involving equal groups, arrays, and measurement quantities, e.g., by using drawings and equations with a symbol for the unknown number to represent the problem."

ChatGPT: Lesson Title: Discovering Multiplication and Division in Everyday Life

Grade Level: 3rd Grade

Duration: 45-minute lesson

Session 1: Understanding Multiplication through Equal Groups and Arrays

Objective:

- Students will learn to use multiplication to solve word problems involving equal groups and arrays.
- Students will understand how to represent multiplication problems with drawings and equations.

Activities:

Introduction to Multiplication (10 minutes):

- Start with a simple explanation of multiplication as repeated addition.
- Use real-life examples, like counting legs on chairs or wheels on cars.

Group Activity: Building Arrays (15 minutes):

- Provide grid paper and small objects (e.g., counters).
- Instruct students to create arrays representing different multiplication facts (e.g., 4 rows of 5 counters).
- Discuss how this visual representation helps understand multiplication.

Exploring Equal Groups (10 minutes):

- Draw or show pictures of equal groups (e.g., bunches of bananas, packs of crayons).
- Have students write multiplication sentences for these groups.

Independent Practice (10 minutes):

- Provide worksheets with problems involving arrays and equal groups.
- Allow students to use drawings to solve these problems.

Conclusion (5 minutes):

- Recap the day's learning.
- Assign simple multiplication problems as homework.

This initial AI-generated lesson plan covers the basics and presents the lesson in a whole-group, teacher-led, teacher-paced instructional model. It does not, however, include differentiation, student agency, or supports and scaffolds to ensure all students are getting what they need to thrive in this lesson. So, we wanted to push ChatGPT to do better.

Keyword Alert!

Differentiation: The process of teachers adapting curriculum, teaching methods, resources, learning activities, and student products to address the diverse needs of individual students and small groups in the classroom to ensure that all students learn effectively, regardless of student variability.

Catlin and Katie: OK. Let's work to develop and differentiate session #1. How can a teacher differentiate the simple explanation of multiplication for students who may have different levels of prior knowledge or skill when it comes to multiplication?

In response to this request, ChatGPT initially provided solid suggestions that nevertheless invoked a language of "Tiers" we both found problematic.

ChatGPT: Differentiating the introduction of multiplication in your lesson plan is essential to cater to students with varying levels of prior knowledge and skill. Here are several strategies a teacher can use to differentiate this part of the lesson:

1. Pre-Assessment and Grouping:

- Pre-Assessment: Conduct a quick pre-assessment, like a short quiz or oral questions, to gauge students' existing knowledge about multiplication.
- Flexible Grouping: Based on the pre-assessment, group students by similar skill levels or mixed abilities, depending on the differentiation strategy you choose.

2. Tiered Instruction:

- Tier 1 (Beginners): For students with limited knowledge of multiplication, start with the very basics of repeated addition (e.g., $2 + 2 + 2 = 6$ as 3×2). Use concrete objects like counters or blocks.
- Tier 2 (Intermediate): For students with some understanding, focus on building arrays and understanding multiplication facts up to 5×5.
- Tier 3 (Advanced): Challenge students who already understand basic multiplication with higher number facts or introduce concepts like commutative property (e.g., 4×3 is the same as 3×4).

3. Visual and Hands-On Learning:

- Use different types of visual aids, like multiplication charts, for students who are visual learners.
- Incorporate hands-on activities, like building arrays with different materials (blocks, counters, paper cut-outs) to cater to kinesthetic learners.

4. Use of Technology:

- Integrate educational technology for students who might be more engaged with digital tools. Apps and online games that teach multiplication can be beneficial, especially for those who are already familiar with the basics.

5. Peer Learning:

- Pair or group students with different levels of understanding. More knowledgeable students can help explain concepts to their peers, reinforcing their own understanding and aiding those who are struggling.

In the example above, ChatGPT highlights the importance of collecting pre-assessment data to inform grouping and the design of targeted instruction at the teacher-led station. These are great suggestions. However, teachers may not know how to differentiate instruction when working with the whole group or what scaffolds and supports would effectively help students at different skill levels or language proficiencies. So, we decided to dig in a bit further, pushing ChatGPT to reimagine this lesson in a structure that would free teachers to meet the needs of specific groups.

One concern we have about ChatGPT's initial effort at differentiation is the use of the word *tiers* when it comes to instruction and its potential confusion with the tiers in multi-tiered systems of supports (MTSS). Generally, Tier 1 is synonymous with instruction provided for all students, recognizing that some students need additional support in small groups. Still, other students may need 1:1 instruction to address lagging skills. Given that this lesson is Tier 1 and provides all students with access to grade-level mathematics instruction, it would be more accurate to call these differentiated groups for targeted instruction.

Keyword Alert!

Multi-tiered system of supports (MTSS): A comprehensive framework that ensures all students engage in the general education curriculum through a flexible approach incorporating three tiers of instructional intensity. This approach is designed to address academic, behavioral, and social-emotional (SEL) needs using evidence-based practices. Central to MTSS is the belief that, with adequate support, every student is capable of grade-level learning. The framework operates on principles of proactivity and prevention, with a schoolwide implementation that requires collaboration among all stakeholders.

Catlin and Katie: Great suggestion to differentiate initial instruction so it is accessible to each group, but your language about tiers is inconsistent with language on multi-tiered systems of support (MTSS) and Response to Intervention (RTI) models. Please change the language and then revise the lesson to help teachers structure this lesson to allow them dedicated time to work with students at each level.

Keyword Alert!

Response to Intervention (RTI) model: A strategy aimed at early identification and support of students with learning and behavior needs, providing interventions at increasing levels of intensity based on students' responsiveness. It integrates continuous monitoring of student progress and data-driven decision-making to adjust the intensity and nature of interventions, with the goal of enhancing student achievement and reducing behavioral problems.

ChatGPT: You're absolutely right about the inconsistency in the use of the term "tiers." To align with the language commonly used in MTSS and RTI models, we should rephrase the differentiation levels. Here's a revised approach to structuring the lesson:

Tiered Instruction Revision:

Instead of using "Tier 1," "Tier 2," and "Tier 3," which might cause confusion with MTSS and RTI terminology, we can use more generic terms to describe the levels of differentiation:

- Foundational Level
- Intermediate Level
- Advanced Level

Here's the revised lesson structure.

Introduction (10 minutes):

- Begin the lesson with a brief introduction to multiplication as a concept.
- Explain to the students that they will be working on multiplication but at different levels based on their readiness.
- Mention that there are three levels: Foundational, Intermediate, and Advanced.

Group Activities (20 minutes):

- Divide the students into three groups, with each group assigned to one of the levels based on their pre-assessment or prior knowledge.
- Each group spends about 6–7 minutes at each station.
- Assign each group to a different station or activity corresponding to their level:
  - Foundational Level: Work on repeated addition and basic multiplication using concrete objects like counters or blocks.
  - Intermediate Level: Focus on building arrays and practicing multiplication facts up to 5×5.

- Advanced Level: Engage in more challenging multiplication activities, such as higher number facts or exploring concepts like the commutative property.

Teacher Support (15 minutes):

- While students are engaged in their respective activities, the teacher rotates among the stations, spending about 6–7 minutes with each group, providing targeted instruction and support at each level.

Wrap-up (5 minutes):

- Gather the students back together as a whole class.
- Review key concepts and takeaways from each level.

This iteration from ChatGPT demonstrates a thoughtful approach to differentiation, moving away from potentially confusing tiered language and instead categorizing activities into foundational, intermediate, and advanced levels. We appreciated the structure provided for group activities and the inclusion of teacher support time, which allows for targeted instruction. However, there are still areas that could be refined. For example, the suggested timing for rotating between stations may need to be adjusted to ensure students have adequate time to engage with the material meaningfully. Additionally, while the group activities are well structured, further differentiation is needed to account for varying language proficiencies and specific learning needs. Based on this reflection, we prompted ChatGPT with the following.

Catlin and Katie: We think 6–7 minutes is not nearly enough time to work with each group for the teacher-led station. Since this is a third-grade math block, a teacher will likely have 60–90 minutes for this lesson. Given that new timeframe, once the whole-group introduction is presented, we think the teacher will need the rest of the class period to work with small groups in the rotation on differentiated instruction, guided practice, and support. We figure they'll need 15–20 minutes with each small group. Can you design a three-station rotation that allows the teacher to work with each group while also ensuring the other groups have tasks appropriate to this standard (even if they do not begin with the teacher)? Please incorporate some of your suggestions above about visual and hands-on learning for the offline station, use of technology for the online station, and peer learning.

Keyword Alert!

The station rotation model: A blended learning model in which students rotate between learning activities that include a teacher-led station, online station, and offline station; however, the total number of stations may vary. The goal of this model is to provide teachers with dedicated time to work with small groups, differentiating instruction, modeling, feedback, and support. Students also have more control over the pace and path of their learning at the online and offline stations.

ChatGPT: Absolutely, with a 60–90 minute math block, you can structure a more in-depth rotation that allows for 15–20 minutes at each station. Here's a redesigned three-station rotation:

Lesson Structure for Extended Tiered Instruction Rotation

Whole-Class Introduction (10 minutes):

- Begin with a whole-class introduction to multiplication, setting the foundation for all students.

Station Rotations (3 stations × 20 minutes each = 60 minutes):

- Divide the class into three groups based on their skill levels (foundational, intermediate, advanced).

Station 1: Teacher-Led Instruction (20 minutes per group): Interactive teaching, guided practice, and immediate feedback.

- Foundational: Introduce basic multiplication concepts, demonstrate using concrete materials (counters, blocks).

- Intermediate: Work on multiplication problems, introduce simple word problems.
- Advanced: Challenge with more complex word problems, introduce concepts like properties of multiplication.

Station 2: Hands-On and Visual Learning (20 minutes): Students work individually or in pairs, creating visual representations of multiplication problems.

- Use grid paper for creating arrays.
- Manipulatives for building and visualizing multiplication (e.g., lego blocks, counters).
- Drawing multiplication scenarios.

Station 3: Technology-Integrated Learning and Peer Collaboration (20 minutes): Students work individually on tech-based activities but collaborate and discuss with peers, facilitating peer learning.

- Use tablets or computers with educational multiplication games and apps.
- Peer-teaching activities where students explain concepts to each other.
- Online quizzes or interactive worksheets.

Conclusion and Reflection (5–10 minutes):

- Regroup and have a brief discussion about what was learned.
- Students can share something new they discovered or explain a concept they found interesting.

In this response, ChatGPT offers a more realistic and practical approach to timing, allowing for deeper engagement and more focused instruction with fifteen to twenty minutes at each station. The breakdown of activities at each station—teacher-led instruction, hands-on and visual learning, and technology-integrated learning with peer collaboration—provides a well-rounded structure that caters to different learning needs. However, we still need to ensure that each station includes specific scaffolds and supports.

Catlin and Katie: Now we are cooking! To further develop this lesson structure for extended differentiated instruction rotation, can you suggest specific scaffolds and support that teachers could provide students at each station to support groups at different levels or language proficiencies?

ChatGPT: Certainly! Providing scaffolds and support is crucial for catering to students at different levels and language proficiencies. Below are specific strategies for each station:

Station 1: Teacher-Led Instruction

- Foundational Support:
  - Visual Aids: Use visual aids like number lines, multiplication charts, and pictorial representations.
  - Concrete Examples: Start with concrete objects (e.g., counters, blocks) to demonstrate multiplication as repeated addition.
  - Simple Language: Use clear, simple language and repeat instructions.
  - Step-by-Step Guidance: Break down problems into smaller, manageable steps.
- Intermediate Support:
  - Guided Questions: Use guided questioning to lead students to find answers themselves.
  - Graphic Organizers: Provide graphic organizers or templates for solving word problems.
  - Language Support: For English Language Learners (ELLs), provide key vocabulary words in advance and use sentence frames to help them articulate their understanding.
- Advanced Support:
  - Challenging Problems: Offer more complex word problems and encourage these students to explain their reasoning.
  - Exploration and Inquiry: Prompt students to explore different strategies for solving problems and to explain their thinking.

- ◦ Peer Teaching: Encourage capable students to explain concepts to their peers, reinforcing their own understanding.

Station 2: Hands-On and Visual Learning

- For All Groups
  - ◦ Manipulatives: Provide manipulatives like counters, blocks, or array cards for visual and tactile learning.
  - ◦ Templates and Grids: Offer grid paper and templates for creating arrays and visual models.
  - ◦ Visual Instructions: Use charts or step-by-step visual guides to assist students in completing tasks.
  - ◦ Checklists: Provide simple checklists or flowcharts for problem-solving steps.

Station 3: Technology-Integrated Learning and Peer Collaboration

- For All Groups
  - ◦ Technology Tools: Select apps and games that are adjustable to different proficiency levels.
  - ◦ Collaborative Activities: Design activities that encourage peer interaction and support, like paired problem-solving or group discussions.
  - ◦ Discussion Prompts: Provide discussion prompts or sentence starters to facilitate conversation and reflection among peers.

Additional Supports for Language Proficiency

- Glossary of Terms: Provide a glossary of key math terms in simple language, possibly in students' first languages.
- Visual Vocabulary Lists: Create visual vocabulary lists with pictures representing key terms.
- Language Buddy System: Pair ELLs with language buddies who can help explain concepts and instructions.

ChatGPT's suggestions here provide a solid set of scaffolds and supports. The emphasis on peer-teaching and collaborative activities is particularly valuable, as it encourages students to learn from and support each other, making the lesson plan more inclusive and effective.

Catlin and Katie: The last element we want to add to this lesson is student agency and meaningful choices. Can you provide suggestions for where teachers can build in "would you rather" choices at each station to provide flexible pathways through the learning experience?

ChatGPT: Incorporating "would you rather" choices in each station is a great way to enhance student agency and provide flexible learning pathways. Here are suggestions for each station:

Station 1: Teacher-Led Instruction

- Choice in Problem Solving:
  - "Would you rather solve a multiplication problem using counters or draw it with pictures?"
  - "Would you rather work on a multiplication word problem about animals or sports?"
  - "Would you rather explore multiplication properties with numbers or with a real-world context (like dividing a pizza)?"

Station 2: Hands-On and Visual Learning

- Choice in Activity:
  - "Would you rather build an array with physical objects (like blocks) or create an array on grid paper using colors?"
  - "Would you rather work on creating patterns with multiplication arrays or solving puzzles that involve arranging numbers in an array format?"
- Choice in Learning Method:

◦ Give students the option to work individually, in pairs, or in small groups, depending on their comfort level and preferred learning needs.

Station 3: Technology-Integrated Learning and Peer Collaboration

- Choice in Technology Use:
  ◦ "Would you rather play a multiplication game on a tablet or complete interactive multiplication problems online?"
  ◦ For older or more advanced students: "Would you rather create a short presentation about what you've learned using a computer program or design a quiz for your peers?"
- Choice in Collaboration:
  ◦ "Would you rather discuss your solutions with a peer or teach a multiplication concept to a small group?"
  ◦ Provide an option for students to either engage in peer review of their work or collaborate on a joint project.

When provided with a simple math standard, ChatGPT generated a clear and straightforward whole-group, teacher-led lesson—the same type of lesson we see in classrooms every week. We spent seven minutes pushing ChatGPT to differentiate the lesson, generate scaffolds to support learners at different skill levels or language proficiencies, and build in student agency with simple "would you rather" choices. The result is a lesson that is designed to meet the diversity of needs in a classroom more effectively.

Let's review! Here is a quick overview of the process we just demonstrated!

Step 1: Insert a grade-level standard and request a lesson designed to meet that standard.

Step 2: Ask AI to differentiate the instruction for groups at different levels (e.g., foundational, intermediate, advanced).

Step 3: Tell AI we want that differentiated instruction to happen at a teacher-led station in a rotation and ask AI to generate an offline station that's hands-on and involves peer learning and an online station that includes technology.

Step 4: Request that AI provide recommendations for how to scaffold and support students at different levels and with varied language proficiencies.

Step 5: Ask AI to provide examples of "would you rather" choices we can add to this rotation to create flexible pathways.

Voilà! A more equitable and student-centered lesson in a matter of minutes!

As this AI-infused lesson plan exemplifies, we need to think of AI as a powerful thought partner, inspiring us to design with purpose and creativity in a fraction of the time this would otherwise take. Whenever we work with AI, the key is to ask good questions and engineer prompts that help AI understand what to prioritize in its design work. As you begin to engage with AI, here are some important questions to keep in mind:

- How can we use AI to help us develop pre-assessments, remove barriers, and differentiate lessons more effectively to meet the diverse needs, skill levels, and learning preferences in our classes?
- How can we lean on AI to provide students with more agency, meaningful choices, and flexible pathways through the learning experience?
- How can we ask AI to generate exemplars, scaffolds, and other supports to ensure all students—and our students, in particular—can access the learning experience?

- How can we leverage AI to find ways to make learning more interesting and relevant for our students?

AI can make an intentional educator almost superhuman in their ability to design effective and equitable lessons, but we must stay mentally engaged in the process. As great as AI-powered education tools are, they don't know our students like we do. As AI technology advances, the human part of the work we do designing and facilitating learning is what will make us relevant in education.

Who This Book Is For

In an era when AI is rapidly reshaping our world, some people in education may feel apprehensive about integrating it into their practice. However, understanding and utilizing AI can help educators design equitable and student-centered learning experiences that not only engage but also empower learners.

We wrote this book to support educators in leveraging the power of AI in the service of strong pedagogical practices that ensure all students make progress toward standards-aligned educational goals—and that they develop into more self-aware and confident learners. We want teachers to feel assured when using these tools to embrace instructional models that allow them to work alongside their students, create flexible pathways through the learning experiences, and provide the necessary support and scaffolds for their learners.

With this book, we want to demystify the integration of AI in education, guiding educators and helping them harness its power to design cohesive units and blended lessons, to maximize engagement, and to position students at the forefront of the learning process. Time is the biggest barrier most teachers face when it comes to their design work. AI breaks down this barrier, enabling teachers to design and facilitate more effective, equitable, and inclusive learning experiences in a fraction of the time.

The primary audiences for this book are teachers, instructional coaches, school leaders, and professors in teacher credential programs. Professors are the teachers of the next generation of educators, so they play a pivotal role in shaping how emerging teachers perceive and incorporate technology in their classrooms. Instructional coaches and leaders will find this book a useful resource in supporting teachers to elevate their design work. We provide practical strategies for layering differentiation, scaffolds, student agency, and inquiry into traditional lessons and district-adopted curriculums. Beyond these immediate applications, though, this book also offers a comprehensive framework for integrating AI into the design process, highlighting a clear design pathway incorporating innovative strategies and best practices. It provides professors with current and relevant examples demonstrating AI's application and value in designing and facilitating student-centered learning experiences.

How This Book Is Organized

We want to support teachers in their work designing lessons that challenge students within their zones of proximal development, fostering an environment where they are questioning, exploring, and seeking answers. In turn, we want students to build confidence in their ability to make decisions and reflect on their efforts, overcoming challenges and recognizing their personal growth.

In this book, we integrate established design frameworks to create a more comprehensive approach and expand our focus. Instead of considering just what we teach and how we teach, we include who we teach and the type of learners we aim to cultivate. Our journey begins with Grant Wiggins and Jay McTighe's Understanding by Design (UbD) framework, utilizing backward design to shift our focus from content to learning outcomes. Backward design helps teachers clarify the learning destination and effectively design assessments and learning pathways to ensure students reach those desired outcomes.

Keyword Alert!

Understanding by design (UbD): A framework developed by Grant Wiggins and Jay McTighe that emphasizes backward design, starting with the end goals of learning in mind. UbD shifts the focus from teaching to learning by first identifying desired results or learning outcomes and then planning the assessments and learning pathway or curriculum that align with these goals. This approach ensures that instruction is purposefully directed toward meaningful and measurable student achievements.

Next, we leverage UDL and blended learning to remove barriers and create flexible pathways for students to acquire information, make meaning, and transfer their learning. Once our lessons are universally designed, the third step in the framework emphasizes the teacher's responsiveness. Despite our best efforts, students will encounter challenges and need support, so this step focuses on adapting instruction to meet the needs that arise during the learning process.

Finally, we conclude the design pathway with a focus on cultivating resilient learners who are self-aware, perseverant, adaptable, and able to enjoy strong relationships and social support. This step involves incorporating elements that help students develop the skills necessary to thrive long after they leave our classrooms.

Accordingly, each chapter of *Elevating Educational Design with AI* explores a sequential step of educators' work in designing accessible, inclusive, and equitable learning experiences, highlighting how they can employ AI to create universally designed blended learning environments anchored in strong pedagogical practices. This book builds on our previous ones, where student-led learning and decision-making were key, and it encourages teachers to craft lessons that compel students to engage deeply and thoughtfully in their learning journeys.

Each chapter follows a similar format:

- **Storytime!** As in previous books, we start with an engaging anecdote or story that illustrates a personal connection with the topic of the chapter.

- **Strong pedagogical practices:** We make the case for how educators can improve their instructional design, shifting from one-size-fits-all learning experiences to incorporating strong pedagogical practices to better meet the needs of all students. We will anchor these design strategies in blended learning and UDL.

- **Leveraging AI:** We help teachers to understand how they can leverage the power of AI to put blended learning and the principles at the heart of UDL into practice every day in the classroom. We discuss learning models that allow teachers to work alongside students while encouraging learners to have more autonomy and agency. Our goal is to help teachers create classrooms in which students have the skills and support necessary to share the responsibility for learning. That is only possible if we invest time and energy into our design work, but we can save some of that time by using AI as a tool.

- **One-sentence summary:** Each chapter features a summary that presents the big takeaways.

- **Reflect and discuss:** We will provide prompts to help you think deeply about the chapter's content, connect it to your practice, and share your learning with your colleagues.

- **Time to apply!** Finally, we've included an action item at the end of each chapter. This activity is designed to help you put what you're learning into practice. It will challenge you to take what you learned and immediately create something you can use with students.

One-Sentence Summary

By combining a comprehensive design framework with the power of AI, educators can create equitable, student-centered learning experiences that truly meet the diverse needs of every learner.

Reflect and Discuss

1. How do you currently design lessons? What is your process like? Do you use an adopted curriculum? If so, how much flexibility do you have to modify that curriculum?

2. How did our interaction with ChatGPT in this chapter underscore the need for teachers to have a deep understanding of pedagogical principles to effectively utilize AI in lesson planning?

3. In what ways did our interaction illustrate that AI should be a complement to, rather than a replacement for, a teacher's pedagogical skills?

4. What are the potential benefits and drawbacks of using AI to design lessons that cater to different learning needs, language proficiencies, and cultural backgrounds?

CHAPTER 1

An AI-Enhanced Design Framework

Just a List of Books?

Catlin When I was hired in 2003 to teach English language arts at Windsor High School, a public school located in Northern California that serves a diverse population of students, I was handed a photocopied list of books. The only directive I received as a new teacher was to select and teach six texts each year and cover the standards.

I remember staring at the blurry, off-center photocopied page and thinking, *Wait, this is it? This is all I get?* I had no school-adopted curriculum other than a handful of dusty old anthologies left by the previous teacher. I didn't have vocabulary workbooks from which to draw grade-level words. No nice, neat grammar lessons with handouts for review. No beautifully written prompts from someone far smarter than a recently graduated twenty-three-year-old with her teaching credential. I felt wildly unprepared to whip up an entire unit of study.

So, I did what a lot of English teachers do: I anchored each of my units in the text we were reading. We had a *Lord of the Flies* unit, a *The Joy Luck Club* unit, an *Of Mice and Men* unit . . . You get the picture.

I pulled a list of ten challenging words from each text for our weekly vocabulary lessons. Often, these were words even I found challenging, like *assuage* from the first chapter of *To Kill a Mockingbird*. I had never used this word, but for some reason, I thought it was critical that my fourteen- and fifteen-year-old students understand and practice using it. (My sincerest apologies to my early students!) With my reading and vocabulary taken care of, I knew I needed to incorporate grammar. So, I bought an eighth-grade grammar book online that provided daily lessons for all 180-plus days of my school year. There were no high school grammar books with quick lessons, so I figured eighth grade was close enough and would have to work!

As a brand-new teacher with no instructional materials, I was in survival mode. I realize now that the problem was not simply that I did not have instructional materials; I didn't have any kind of structure to guide my design work. It's hard to imagine now as I work with graduate students preparing to enter the teaching profession, but a design framework had not been part of my teacher training program. I had not been taught how to construct a pedagogically sound unit of study aligned with grade-level standards. Yes, I knew I had standards to teach, but I was using them to guide the design of individual lessons or activities, not to construct an overarching instructional strategy.

If I were a new teacher today, my reality would be very different. Artificial intelligence makes it exponentially easier to generate lessons and learning activities aligned to grade-level subject-area standards. Yet without a design framework, I would still be churning out daily lessons without a clear sense of whether those lessons were moving my students toward learning goals and objectives. And just like during my first four or five years of teaching, I would not be designing learning experiences with accessibility, inclusivity, or equity in mind.

> **Keyword Alert!**
>
> **Design:** In this context, *design* refers to the intentional planning and structuring of educational content, emphasizing both form and function. It involves combining lessons, activities, and assessments into cohesive and adaptive instructional plans. Effective design ensures that all learners can reach the desired learning outcomes by aligning these educational components with grade-level standards and creating a framework that addresses the diverse needs of students. The form pertains to how the unit is organized and structured, while the function ensures that each lesson effectively contributes to students mastering the set learning goals.

In this chapter, we present a comprehensive design framework that guides teachers through the design process, utilizing AI as a resource to create learning experiences that meet their students' diverse needs. This framework not only helps craft standards-aligned lessons and units but also emphasizes accessibility, inclusivity, and equity—key elements often neglected when teachers navigate the design process without sufficient guidance. By providing a clear design pathway and practical tips for leveraging AI at each step, we aim to ensure success even for those who, like me back in 2003, may not have access to a comprehensive curriculum. Ultimately, this design framework empowers teachers to transform the overwhelming task of lesson planning into an intentional and impactful practice that truly benefits all learners.

Strong Pedagogical Practices

We know that each year, the spectrum of need in classrooms only widens, with new and emerging needs such as increased mental health and behavioral challenges, a rise in multilingual learners, and advances in emerging technology being a few examples. This diversity of needs demands more of educators. In their book *Teaching Models:*

Designing Instruction for 21st Century Learners, Clare Kilbane and Natalie Milman emphasize the teacher's role as a designer of learning experiences in an increasingly diverse and technology-rich educational landscape:

> Regardless of what you teach or where you teach, your success as an educator in the 21st century depends on your ability to design effective instruction for those you teach. Such instruction addresses the individual and shared learning needs of a diverse population of students as they work to master content area learning and the skills required for life in our fast-paced, technology-driven, global society. Contemporary educators find themselves surrounded by an unprecedented variety of powerful teaching resources. However, these resources—whether materials, models, strategies, or technologies—are effective only if teachers know when and how to use them.[1]

Kilbane and Milman's design work, which we like to compare to the work of an architect, is cognitively demanding. It demands that, as teachers, we *really* know our students and use data strategically to identify and meet their changing needs. As an architect of learning experiences, it is our job to draft a blueprint or create a structure for the lesson that positions students to be active agents leading the learning. This work to prepare for class is essential if teachers are going to escape the front of the room and spend their precious class time working directly with students to ensure that they are all progressing toward firm, standards-aligned learning goals.

We regularly work with teachers who do not invest significant time designing lessons, much less lessons that integrate the principles of UDL and blended learning models. And it's because these teachers are already stretched too thin. However, we would argue that refocusing one's attention on design work is ultimately the best way to enhance effectiveness and efficiency in the long run. When teachers do *not* invest time in their design work, the outcome is often a whole-group lesson that positions the teacher at the front of the room talking while students are relegated to listening, taking notes, and then moving on to individual practice. By contrast, the more time a teacher spends designing intentional, student-centered learning experiences, the more time they get back in the classroom to support learning.

The more time a teacher spends designing intentional, student-centered learning experiences, the more time they get back in the classroom to support learning.

Thanks to the advent of AI tools like ChatGPT, the time crunch that might otherwise prevent educators from employing strong design frameworks has been significantly eased. Before AI, it took significantly longer to design a lesson that allowed students to lead their own learning—asking questions, exploring resources, engaging in conversation, and using each other as valuable resources in the classroom. Now, AI provides a powerful design partner that can help teachers with this process.

District-adopted curriculums can also impact our perceptions of ourselves as designers of learning experiences because we are using, in part, materials developed by someone else. To refine the analogy, consider how using an adopted curriculum is akin to purchasing a well-designed tract home: while structurally sound and thoughtfully planned, that home may not include custom features tailored to individual buyers. In the same way, a teacher utilizing high-quality instructional resources has a solid foundation for standards-based instruction, yet they may need significant adjustments to ensure that content meets the needs of diverse students. This process of refinement and adaptation demonstrates the dynamic nature of teaching. Just as a house might undergo renovations to better suit its owners, even a high-quality, flexible curriculum benefits from a teacher's customizations to fit the specific educational landscape of their classroom. AI allows us to do just that.

As a design tool, AI can also help us to confront the inevitable shortcomings of curriculums that have not been thoughtfully designed. An American Instructional Resources Survey found that a higher percentage of teachers "reported regularly using new, standards-aligned curriculum materials in the 2021–2022 school year than during the previous two school years."[2] The same report revealed that even though teachers regularly used new instructional materials in class, they felt those materials were falling short of meeting student needs. In fact, half of the teachers surveyed "cited moderate or major unmet needs for curriculum materials that engage students and for materials that better meet the needs of students on both ends of the achievement spectrum."[3] That shortfall makes sense: students who are struggling and need additional scaffolding and support, as well as students who excel and are ready for further challenge, are unlikely to get what they need from a whole-group lesson that provides the same experience, teacher time, and energy inputs to everyone.

Equity is only possible when we acknowledge that individual learners need individual inputs to work toward the same outputs and outcomes. If we want to design equitable learning experiences, we must design with individual students in mind.

> ### *Keyword Alert!*
>
> **Equity:** The principle and practice of ensuring that each student receives the targeted support they need to succeed, considering their unique circumstances and requirements. This is the opposite of providing one-size-fits-all support. Unlike equality, which implies treating every student the same, equity acknowledges that some students require additional support and tailored instruction to achieve comparable growth and positive learning outcomes. Equity is only possible when we acknowledge that individual learners need individual inputs to work toward the same outputs and outcomes. If we want to design equitable learning experiences, we must design with individual students in mind.

We cannot teach equitably when we teach from a place of improvisation. Faced with deficient materials, teachers often do what Catlin did early in her career, cobbling lessons together with the depersonalized resources available online or purchasing materials prepared by other educators via a site like Teachers Pay Teachers. These materials may meet short-term needs, but they are less likely to be part of a cohesive, standards-aligned unit capable of meeting the requirements of twenty-first-century learners. Such a student body is characterized by Kilbane and Milman as including the following:

- Individuals with "unique experiences, values, and interests"
- Students who are more culturally and linguistically diverse
- Learners who are commonly identified as possessing "physical, cognitive, emotional, or behavioral characteristics that are significantly different"
- Students growing up in a digital era[4]

These characteristics of twenty-first-century students demand a design approach that honors the increasing diversity in classrooms and features the thoughtful integration of technology to teach students how to learn using the tools they'll have access to in their lives beyond school.

There are a variety of models in education intended to guide a teacher's design work to meet the needs of today's students: UbD, UDL, and the Collaborative for Academic, Social, and Emotional Learning (CASEL) framework for SEL. Each of these approaches is worth careful consideration, so in the next section, we'll unpack them to highlight their benefits to you and to your students. However, we know that fully integrating these pedagogical principles into your own classroom isn't easy. So, we'll present a new AI-enhanced design framework that we've devised to guide you in leveraging the power of artificial intelligence. Our framework will empower you to craft cohesive units comprising universally designed, blended lessons that will help students develop the metacognitive and SEL skills necessary to become resilient learners who enjoy strong relationships with other members of the learning community.

Understanding by Design (UbD)

UbD provides a clear, structured approach to curriculum planning that prioritizes student learning outcomes over content delivery. By starting with the end in mind, UbD addresses the common problem of misalignment between teaching activities, learning goals, and assessments, ensuring that every aspect of instruction leads to meaningful, measurable student achievement. This approach helps educators focus on the ultimate learning objectives, making their teaching more effective and impactful.

Developed by Grant Wiggins and Jay McTighe, UbD "offers a three-stage curriculum unit design process based on the idea that teaching is a means to an end, and curriculum planning precedes instruction."[5] This backward design approach strives to shift the focus of our design work from teaching to learning, prioritizing learning objectives over the topic, texts, or specific teaching methods.

In their book *Understanding by Design*, Wiggins and McTighe point out that "too many teachers focus on the *teaching* and not the *learning*. They spend most of their time thinking about what they will do, what materials they will use, and what they will ask students to do rather than first considering what the learner will need to accomplish the learning goals."[6] Wiggins and McTighe encourage educators and curriculum writers to shift from a content-focused approach to a results-focused one that starts with the end in mind and works backward. In essence, Wiggins and McTighe advise that we should avoid what Catlin did early in her career when she planned her lesson according to the book she was going to teach instead of first identifying what students needed to understand by the end of the unit.

Backward design entails three major steps. The first involves clearly articulating a unit's desired result or destination. Wiggins and McTighe encourage educators to ask the following questions during this first stage of design: What do we want students to know, understand, or be able to do? What is the ultimate transfer we seek as a result of this unit? What enduring understandings are desired? What essential questions will be explored in-depth and provide focus to all learning?[7] For example, a history teacher might aim for students to understand the impact of historical events on contemporary society and be able to create a multimedia presentation that connects past events to current issues. In a science class, a teacher might aim for students to understand the principles of ecosystems and apply this knowledge by designing a sustainable garden.

These questions help educators and curriculum designers to identify standards-aligned learning objectives that will guide our work in constructing a cohesive unit. As such, unpacking standards to tease out stated and implied ideas or concepts, as well as skills and real-world performances, is a critical part of this initial step.

Once the designer has clearly articulated the desired result, the next step that Wiggins and McTighe suggest is to decide on an assessment strategy for the unit. In other words, what evidence can help us to determine how much progress students make toward the desired results or learning objectives? We need to consider how students can demonstrate their ability to transfer or apply their learning. For example, if the desired result is for students to understand the principles and structure of argumentative writing, an appropriate assessment strategy might include having them write and present or record an argumentative speech on a topic of their choice. This performance task allows students to apply their learning by crafting arguments, using rhetorical devices, and presenting their ideas coherently, providing clear evidence of their understanding and skill.

Moving directly from the first step (articulating the desired result) to this second step (deciding on assessment evidence) ensures that our learning goals and assessment strategies are perfectly aligned before we begin to work on the instructional path, or sequences of lessons, we need to implement to move students toward a desired result. This learning pathway must help students acquire the necessary information, engage in meaning-making activities, and demonstrate their ability to transfer or apply their learning.

To extend our example above on argumentative writing, teachers might include several key elements in the learning pathway. The pathway could begin with lessons on the fundamentals of argumentative writing, such as understanding claims, evidence, reasoning, and how to structure a coherent argument. Analyzing strong examples of argumentative writing, like essays, opinion pieces, and debates, can help students identify key techniques and strategies. Scaffolded writing exercises can then allow students to practice specific components of argumentative writing, such as developing a strong thesis statement, constructing logical arguments, and effectively using evidence and counterarguments. Incorporating group activities where students brainstorm and critique each other's arguments can provide valuable feedback and suggestions for improvement. Using graphic organizers can help students plan and structure their argumentative essays, ensuring they include all necessary components and maintain a logical flow.

Backward design provides a structure for thoughtful unit planning. It helps an educator or curriculum designer approach their work from that fifty-foot view before diving into the design of individual lessons or learning experiences. This approach to design ensures that every lesson and activity is aligned with overarching learning goals, leading to more coherent and focused instruction. Additionally, by clearly defining desired outcomes from the start, teachers can create assessments that accurately measure student understanding and progress. This not only enhances the effectiveness of teaching but also promotes deeper, more meaningful learning experiences for students.

Universal Design for Learning (UDL)

Inspired by Universal Design as applied in architecture, UDL is focused on designing rigorous classroom environments that are accessible to, and engaging for, all students. This inclusive approach ensures every student has the opportunity to access grade-level instruction with their peers, regardless of their needs, much like how well-designed buildings meet the needs of all people. UDL is backed by decades of brain-based research arguing that for our students to learn, we need to activate three neural networks in their brains: the affective network, the recognition network, and the strategic network. These three brain networks align with the three principles of

UDL, which state that we must design multiple means of engagement, representation, and expression.

This focus on fostering learner agency aligns seamlessly with the need to engage the affective network in educational design, which emphasizes the "why" of learning and ensures that lessons resonate with students' real-world experiences and needs. All too often, lessons presume, rather than consider, students' real-world education needs. To pay attention, students need learning opportunities that are relevant, authentic, and meaningful for them.

In a UDL-based classroom, a history teacher might design a unit on the civil rights movement by integrating students' interests and real-world experiences. Instead of simply lecturing on historical events, the teacher could invite students to explore how the principles of the civil rights movement relate to current social justice issues they are passionate about. To learn more about these topics, students could choose to research local civil rights history, interview community members, or analyze primary source documents. They could then choose a project-based way to share their learning, such as a multimedia presentation, podcast series, or documentary film that connects past and present struggles for equality. This approach not only covers the required content but also makes the learning experience relevant and meaningful by connecting it to students' lives, activating the affective network and fostering deeper engagement and motivation.

The recognition network is responsible for the "what" of learning; it allows students to access relevant content and concepts that help them process and retain new information. This network must be activated with multiple means of representation so that students can make *sense* of the information they learn. We tend to think of direct instruction as the "what" of learning. However, when teachers present information, we often use a single representation and provide the same lesson to all students, lecturing, playing a video, conducting a lab, teaching vocabulary, and so forth. Even when we think we are being creative by asking students to listen to a podcast or read a series of social media posts, we are still providing only a single representation method. When we provide multiple means of representation, our students can choose the resources that best match their strengths, their needs, and the lesson's purpose, all while working toward the same firm goals.

For example, a science teacher might introduce the topic of ecosystems by offering students various ways to access the content. Students could watch a documentary, read articles, explore inter-active simulations, or participate in hands-on experiments. They could also listen to podcasts or engage in group discussions. By providing these multiple means of representation, students can select the method that best suits their learning preferences, helping them understand and retain the information more effectively.

Finally, activating the strategic network entails engaging the "how" of learning. Once students are interested in authentic learning outcomes, and once they have learned the information using the best method for their needs, they must express their understanding in an authentic assessment that is aligned with the firm goals of the lesson. To achieve this, multiple means of expression must be available that will activate the strategic network. Traditionally, students are asked to share their understanding using one-size-fits-all assessments. For example, many teachers assess students by providing the same multiple-choice tests, worksheets, writing assignments, and projects. There is no opportunities for student autonomy, which is critical for deeper learning.

As an example, in a universally designed English/language arts classroom, a teacher might assess students' understanding of a short, profound text, such as an excerpt from *The Water Dancer* by Ta-Nehisi Coates. Instead of requiring all students to write an essay on how the characters interact over the course of the text, the teacher could offer multiple ways for students to demonstrate their knowledge. Students could choose to write an analytical essay, create a visual art piece, develop a multimedia presentation, perform a dramatic reenactment, or compose a song. This variety in assessment methods respects students' diverse strengths and preferences as they work toward the same goal.

When all three networks of the brain are activated, students are like freshly opened cans of seltzer: they bubble with purpose and motivation because they are working toward authentic goals that challenge them individually. At the same time, they receive support from their teacher, who is available to work with students individually. Students can also collaborate in small groups, and this peer support helps reinforce understanding, encourages different perspectives, and fosters a collaborative learning environment where students feel empowered and connected.

Blended learning and UDL create a powerful synergy that makes it more manageable for teachers to implement UDL principles in their classrooms. Blended learning models, such as the station rotation model, flipped classroom, and playlist model, free the teacher from the front of the room, allowing them to work alongside individuals and small groups to meet specific needs. This flexibility is essential for putting UDL into practice, as it enables teachers to provide multiple means of engagement, representation, and expression while also tailoring instruction to each student.

By leveraging blended learning, teachers can prioritize data-informed design, student agency, and differentiation—critical components of UDL. For example, in a station rotation model, the teacher has dedicated time to work with small groups differentiating instruction, modeling sessions, feedback, and supports. Students also enjoy more control over the pace at which they work and the path they take through an activity, making key decisions about how they engage with the content, make meaning, and apply their learning.

Ultimately, the integration of blended learning and UDL creates an inclusive and dynamic learning environment where all students can thrive. By using blended learning models to implement UDL principles, teachers can ensure that their instructional design is both flexible and student-centered, leading to more effective and equitable learning experiences for all.

Collaborative for Academic, Social, and Emotional Learning (CASEL)

Many students struggle with developing essential social and emotional skills, which are critical for their overall well-being and academic success. The CASEL framework equips educators and communities with a comprehensive set of strategies designed to foster the development of SEL learning skills. It also strives to support educators and educational institutions in cultivating learning environments that are specifically designed to support students in their learning and overall development.

The CASEL framework[8] focuses on five core competencies that are at the heart of social-emotional learning: self-awareness, self-management, social awareness, relationship skills, and responsible decision-making. As research has established, these skills are critical to a student's personal development and ability to establish and maintain positive relationships and academic achievement.[9] Accordingly, schools that integrate SEL skills experience a significant improvement in students' skills, behaviors, attitudes, relationships with peers, and ability to function in school (e.g., attend class and complete homework).[10] Unfortunately, SEL skills are often treated as an add-on instead of being woven into the fabric of a student's academic experience. These skills are critical to cultivating confident learners who can navigate a learning environment where they are given more control over their experience.

> ### *Keyword Alert!*
>
> **CASEL framework:** A comprehensive model that outlines key competencies for social and emotional learning (SEL). It focuses on five core areas: self-awareness, self-management, social awareness, relationship skills, and responsible decision-making. By integrating these competencies into educational practices, the CASEL framework aims to promote students' academic success, emotional well-being, and positive social interactions, preparing them for success in school and life.

One effective CASEL-based teaching approach is integrating SEL into existing academic subjects through project-based learning (PBL). For example, in an eighth-grade science class, students work on a project about environmental sustainability. Throughout the project, the teacher intentionally incorporates self-awareness and self-management by having students set personal learning goals and reflect on their progress. At the beginning of the unit, students complete self-assessments to identify their strengths and areas for growth.

As part of the project, students collaborate in diverse teams to research local environmental issues and propose sustainable solutions. This collaboration requires them to practice social awareness and develop relationship skills, including effective communication, active listening, and conflict resolution. The teacher facilitates discussions on how to navigate group dynamics, share responsibilities, and respect diverse perspectives, helping students build strong interpersonal skills. Responsible decision-making is integrated into the process, and students evaluate the potential impact of their proposed solutions, considering ethical implications, sustainability, and the well-being of their community. This critical thinking aspect helps students understand the importance of making informed, responsible choices. This example demonstrates how the core competencies in the CASEL framework can be integrated into the work students do—and how this integration makes that work more meaningful and impactful.

Similarly, the core competencies identified in the CASEL framework reinforce the chief benefits of UDL and blended learning, and vice versa. So, if UDL and blended learning invite students to take more ownership of their experiences by making key decisions about their learning, then CASEL helps us to cultivate learners who are resourceful, strategic, motivated, and self-aware. In the case of blended learning, employing various technology-enhanced instructional models helps us to shift some decisions to students, giving them more control over the time, place, pace, and path of learning. That flexibility demands that our students be equipped to manage their own behavior without much direction from us. They also must be able to work independently and in concert with peers, which requires that they make responsible decisions and have positive relationships with the other members of their learning communities.

Leveraging AI: An AI-Enhanced Design Framework

Instead of talking about these various frameworks as siloed approaches to designing dynamic, student-centered learning experiences, we want to show you how they can work in concert. Together, these frameworks can help teachers move from the fifty-foot view of unit planning down to the ten-foot view of lesson design and, finally, to ground zero—the student experience. As we explained in the introduction, our goal with this book is to help teachers approach educational design with a high level of intentionality, whether you're designing lessons from scratch or adapting high-quality instructional resources. In that light, we propose a new hybrid design framework that integrates many of the ideas from these established educational approaches to create a clear and comprehensive design pathway for teachers—all while using artificial intelligence. Our AI-enhanced design framework will guide you through the process of planning the learning experience strategically while utilizing data to address your students' needs effectively. Additionally, our framework allows you to incorporate SEL components that develop and nurture resilient learners.

> ### *Keyword Alert!*
>
> **Design framework:** A design framework is a structured approach used to guide the planning, development, and implementation of instructional units and lessons. It provides educators with a systematic way to organize their teaching strategies, objectives, and assessments, ensuring that all elements align with desired learning outcomes. By following a design framework, teachers can create more effective, cohesive, and student-centered educational experiences.

In the chapters that follow, we will demonstrate how this framework allows you to leverage AI as a design partner, even while utilizing your state and subject-area standards, or adopted curriculum, as a starting point. Throughout, we'll provide prompts that you can use to interact with AI to produce results that will help you to universally design blended learning models that will shift the focus and workload in your classrooms away one-size-fits-all explicit instruction and toward your capable learners.

Our AI-enhanced design framework is composed of four steps, as pictured in figure 1.1. As the teacher, you begin at the top and work your way down the design path, starting with the overall unit design, moving on to individual lessons, considering your own facilitation practices, and, finally, transforming the student experience.

While chapters 3 through 8 will tackle each step of this AI-enhanced design framework individually, it's worth considering each part of this sequence at the outset so that we can lay some groundwork for the path ahead. It's important to note that, at every step, AI will serve as a powerful thought partner and ally that can help us keep our UbD, UDL, blended learning, and CASEL principles front and center.

Step 1: Identify the Desired Results

Step 1 focuses on using the backward design process to create a comprehensive unit aligned with grade-level and subject-area standards. This is the high-level design needed to create the overall structure of a cohesive unit. The focus of this first step is to ensure that we begin by identifying what students should know, understand, or be able to do at the end of a unit *instead* of starting with *how* we plan to teach or *what* we plan to teach. Those decisions around *how* and *what* happen later, once we have identified the learning goals or objectives. We begin step 1 by selecting target standards for our unit and then articulating the desired results or learning objectives based on those standards. Once the desired results have been articulated, we must decide how we will measure progress toward those learning objectives, selecting a flexible assessment strategy. Because students express and communicate their learning differently, we encourage teachers to prioritize student agency in their assessment strategy whenever possible to ensure all students can effectively share their learning.

AI can play a crucial role in step 1 of the design framework by helping educators identify desired results. It can assist teachers in selecting target standards for their unit by providing relevant standards based on grade level and subject area. AI can also guide teachers through articulating clear learning objectives by offering suggestions and examples aligned with those standards. Additionally, it can help educators brainstorm flexible assessment strategies by recommending various methods to measure student progress, emphasizing the importance of student agency. By leveraging AI, teachers can streamline the initial planning process, ensuring that their unit design is both comprehensive and aligned with educational goals.

Figure 1.1: Tucker and Novak AI-Enhanced Design Framework

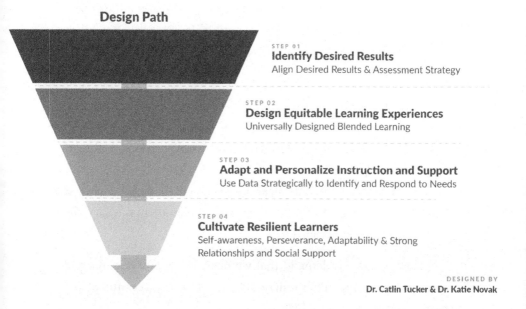

Design Path

STEP 01
Identify Desired Results
Align Desired Results & Assessment Strategy

STEP 02
Design Equitable Learning Experiences
Universally Designed Blended Learning

STEP 03
Adapt and Personalize Instruction and Support
Use Data Strategically to Identify and Respond to Needs

STEP 04
Cultivate Resilient Learners
Self-awareness, Perseverance, Adaptability & Strong
Relationships and Social Support

DESIGNED BY
Dr. Catlin Tucker & Dr. Katie Novak

Step 2: Design Equitable Learning Experiences

Once the learning objectives and assessment strategy are aligned, we move on to step 2 of the design path. Here, we think about the learning pathways we need to establish to ensure *all* our students make progress toward the firm, standards-aligned goals we identify in step 1. At this point, we use UDL and blended learning models—as well as our AI partner—to design student-centered learning experiences that provide flexible pathways through the learning experience. We know that different students will need different levels of support and scaffolding, so the goal with this step is to design lessons that free us to spend time with individual and small groups of students, differentiating and personalizing learning along the way. We also position our students as capable of leading aspects of the learning experience as described in our book *The Shift to Student-Led: Reimagining Classroom Workflows with UDL and Blended Learning.*[11]

The goal at this stage of the design process is to universally design blended lessons to ensure all learners receive the input they need to reach the desired result. To architect lessons that strive to meet the variability in their classes, the teacher must consider the following questions:

- Who am I designing for?
- What are their specific needs and preferences?
- What barriers might prevent them from accessing the learning experience?
- Where can I include meaningful choices to remove barriers?
- What supports and scaffolds would help them navigate the learning experience?

These questions demand that we *really* know our students and consider what they might individually need to be successful. Step 3 helps us dig deeper into this.

Step 3: Adapt and Personalize Instruction and Support

Once we have designed a sequence of lessons we believe will guide our diverse group of learners from the starting point to the desired result, we need to think about how we will collect and use formative assessment data to respond to individual learners' needs as they progress through the learning experience.

Even as we endeavor to provide the necessary support and scaffolding for each student, we know that best-laid plans often take unexpected turns. Students will likely hit unforeseen obstacles, need reteaching, and struggle with a particular skill. That is where we, when freed to interact with students nimbly, can have the biggest impact. We want to ensure that we can embrace our facilitation role and have the time and space to respond to student needs and engage in the human side of this work. Step 3 accomplishes this goal by allowing us to use real-time data and feedback to adapt our teaching strategies, ensuring that each student receives the targeted support they need. This responsive approach not only addresses immediate learning challenges but also fosters a more personalized and effective learning environment.

AI can help teachers in this third step of the design process by analyzing formative assessment data quickly and accurately, identifying patterns and trends that might not be immediately apparent to teachers. It can provide insights into individual student progress and areas of difficulty, helping educators to make informed decisions about when and how to intervene to offer targeted support and adjustments in real time. AI can also help teachers generate specific examples, scaffolds, and other resources to help individual students who need additional support.

Step 4: Cultivate Resilient Learners

The goal of formal education is not for students to become experts at everything; it's for them to become skilled at navigating new learning experiences with confidence! As part of the design process, we must think about how we are helping our students to develop into resilient learners who are self-aware, perseverant, and adaptable people who have strong relationships with teachers and peers. Such students are more likely to have the skills and confidence needed in a self-directed learning environment.

The goal of formal education is not for students to become experts at everything; it's for them to become skilled at navigating new learning experiences with confidence!

At this final step in the design process, we must think about building opportunities for students to develop their metacognitive muscles and hone SEL skills of self-awareness, self-management, and responsible decision-making. As designers of the learning experience, teachers need to integrate these critical skills into lessons, helping students learn how to confidently navigate learning tasks and engage in cooperative collaboration with diverse groups of peers. We must consider how we can leverage practices such as goal-setting, thinking routines, role-playing exercises, self-assessment, and reflective practices to help students develop into resilient learners who understand their strengths and limitations and can advocate for their specific needs as learners.

The Inversion:
From Design Path to Learning Path

It's critical to keep our students focused on developing their ability to learn. We must remember that if they are going to be successful academically, students must develop a clear understanding of themselves as learners so that they can gain confidence in their ability to approach new, complex, and challenging tasks. The time and energy we invest in fostering resilient learners will help students reach the academic results we are working toward.

Accordingly, the beauty of our AI-enhanced design framework is that it not only provides teachers with a clear design path, but when inverted, as pictured in figure 1.2, it depicts the learning pathway that our students will traverse from developing as resilient learners to achieving desired learning outcomes. Let's take a closer look at this inverted version of the learning pathway.

Figure 1.2: Tucker and Novak's Learning Pathway

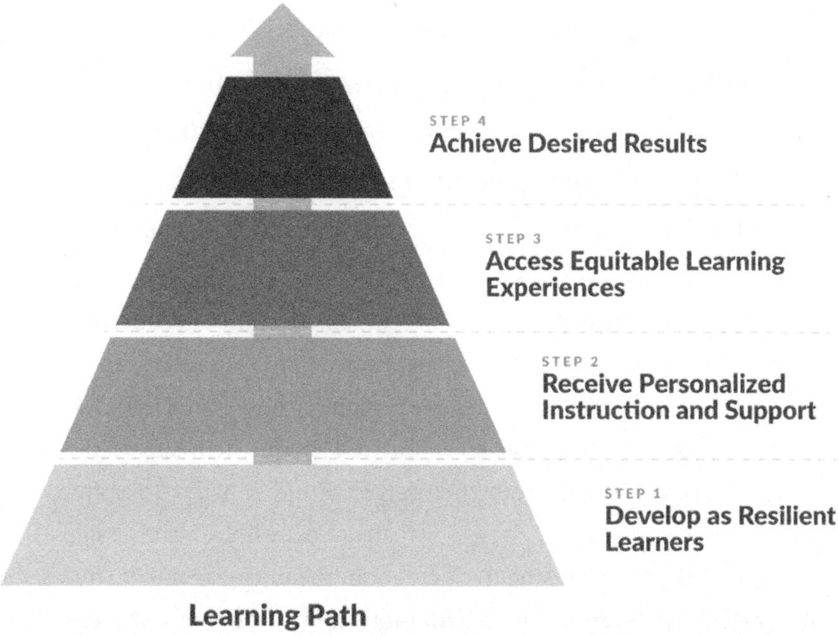

STEP 4
Achieve Desired Results

STEP 3
Access Equitable Learning Experiences

STEP 2
Receive Personalized Instruction and Support

STEP 1
Develop as Resilient Learners

Learning Path

Step 1: Develop as Resilient Learners

The first step of the learning pathway is for students to focus on developing as resilient learners. This isn't a discrete step; resilience in the face of challenges and setbacks must be the foundation of student work in all classrooms. In *The Shift to Student-Led: Reimagining Classroom Workflows with UDL and Blended Learning*, we argue that teachers work too hard for the results they're getting. The traditional approach to teaching creates an unhealthy and unsustainable work-life balance. The only way to correct this imbalance is to teach our students how to share the responsibility for learning with us. Students, in other words, need to act as our learning partners.

We know the traditional approach to teaching creates an unhealthy and unsustainable work-life balance. The only way to correct this imbalance is to teach our students how to share the responsibility for learning with us. Students, in other words, need to act as our learning partners.

The work educators do to help students become more resilient is easy to neglect because it does not appear in the standards or an adopted curriculum. Students need regular opportunities to set goals, engage in self-assessment, and reflect on their experiences in our classes to learn about themselves as individuals. Too often, students jump through a series of instructional hoops and assignments without ever pausing to think about the purpose of that work. If more teachers were working with motivated, resourceful, strategic, and self-aware students, we believe teaching would be more rewarding for everyone involved—teachers and learners!

Step 2: Receive Personalized Instruction and Support

Teacher-student interactions are where the magic happens in classrooms! During lessons, students need their teachers to respond to their individual needs by providing personalized instruction, feedback, and support that ensures they progress toward learning objectives.

Data is one of the best tools teachers have for responding to students' needs and effectively personalizing learning in the classroom. We must use formative assessment data produced by students as they move through lessons and learning experiences. With it, we can employ responsive strategies like pulling small groups or providing real-time feedback and support to make sure all students are getting what they need to make progress.

Research conducted in US elementary classrooms found the quality of interactions was generally low.[12] However, students who have good access to their teachers and enjoy individual interactions with them are more likely to be motivated and academically successful. When teachers universally design lessons with blended learning models, they have the time and space in class to be responsive to individual learners and work alongside them to support their progress.

Teacher-student interactions are also necessary for personalized learning, which is grounded in a partnership between the teacher and the learner. Barbara Bray and Kathleen McClaskey define personalized learning as learner-centered: the student has the best understanding of how they learn, and they can work with the teacher to articulate their learning goals.[13] Personalization attempts to connect the learning experiences with student's interests and passions while seeking to understand how they like to access information (e.g., text, audio, video), how they like to communicate what they know (e.g., speaking, drawing, writing), and how they prefer to engage with content. In addition, according to Bray and McClaskey, personalization engages students in making key decisions about their learning.

The more self-directed learning and self-regulation students are capable of, the easier it is for teachers to design lessons that allow time and space to work directly with individuals or small groups, differentiating instruction and personalizing their experience in the classroom. This is why cultivating resilient learners is the first area of focus in the learning path: it creates the foundation for the rest of the learning.

Step 3: Access Equitable Learning Experiences

Learner variability in education is the norm, not the exception. Classrooms are composed of beautifully diverse groups of learners with different backgrounds, language proficiencies, skills, abilities, interests, preferences, and social-emotional needs. Students are *just different* from one another and, as a result, they learn differently. Despite that reality, most learning experiences and learning environments are not designed with variability in mind.

Barbara Pape, the senior director of the Learner Variability Project, points out that "school systems that use a one-size-fits-all model continue to under-serve nearly all of their students."[14] It's this dominant one-size-fits-all approach to designing learning experiences that inspired us to team up in 2021 to write our first book, *UDL and Blended Learning.* We recognized that the whole-group, teacher-led, teacher-paced lesson was too rigid and inflexible and, ultimately, not serving students or teachers.

Many teachers may believe that designing a single lesson for an entire class is the most efficient and effective approach. However, this method often leads to exhausting, messy, frustrating, and disappointing outcomes. This approach creates barriers rather than learning opportunities, as a significant number of students fail to achieve short-term learning objectives or long-term desired results. Instead of continuing to use class time primarily for transferring information and facilitating a uniform experience, our AI-enhanced design framework prioritizes connecting with our learners. After all, engaging in the human side of teaching—the very reason most educators entered this profession—allows us to make the most of our precious class time and truly impact our students' learning.

To create equitable learning environments, it is essential to understand our students deeply. This includes being proactive in identifying and addressing potential barriers that may hinder their ability to access information, engage in activities, or complete tasks. Thus, our framework emphasizes the importance of providing flexible pathways through a lesson by leveraging technology and prioritizing student agency.

Step 4: Achieve Desired Results

We believe students who are self-aware, perseverant, adaptable, and able to have strong relationships are more likely to thrive academically and reach the desired results. From the student perspective, then, we like to think of the apex of our AI-enhanced design framework as aligned with Maslow's hierarchy of needs. At the very top of Maslow's hierarchy, we can self-actualize or fully realize our potential. For students to reach their academic potential, their more basic needs have to be fulfilled—the need for autonomy, support, and excellent teachers and teaching. By leveraging the AI-enhanced design framework, we can help build a foundation from which students can pursue clear opportunities and pathways to achieve at the highest level possible.

One-Sentence Summary

The AI-enhanced design framework, composed of four steps—identifying desired results, designing equitable learning experiences, adapting and personalizing instruction and support, and cultivating resilient learners—provides a structured approach to planning and implementing student-centered learning, making this level of intentionality sustainable and manageable through the use of AI.

Reflect and Discuss

1. Reflect on the diverse needs of students in your classroom. How do you currently attempt to meet that diversity of needs? How might this AI-enhanced design framework help in addressing these needs more effectively?

2. How do you balance the use of technology with traditional teaching methods in your classroom? What challenges and opportunities does this balance present? How can this blend of online and offline learning help you to create flexible pathways in a lesson or learning experience?

3. What strategies do you currently use to help students be more self-aware, perseverant, adaptable, and able to develop strong relationships with the other members of the learning community?

4. What are your thoughts on establishing a foundation of resilient learners for the learning pathway described in this chapter? How might focusing on this with a higher level of intentionality yield more academically confident and successful learners?

Time to Apply!

1. Let's start this work by completing a self-assessment of a unit you are using this year. Think about your unit in terms of the following elements and rate yourself on a scale of one to five. One indicates that you did not consider this design element and five indicates that you spent significant time considering this design element.

   a) Identifying the desired results, or what students should know or be able to do at the end of the unit.

   b) Designing equitable learning experiences through the lens of UDL and blended learning to give each student what they need to make progress in the unit.

   c) Adapting and personalizing instruction and support as students work by collecting and using formative assessment data.

   d) Cultivating resilient learners who are self-aware, perseverant, adaptable, and able to enjoy strong relationships and social support.

2. Based on your self-assessment, what would you identify as your areas of strength and areas in need of improvement?

3. Set a professional goal for yourself to guide your work as you make your way through this book.

CHAPTER 2:

Mindset Makeover: Adaptive Teaching

Thank Goodness for Pete

Katie I recently completed a master bathroom renovation, a project that turned out to be far more time-consuming than anticipated. Thankfully, I didn't have to sweat over daily decisions because of my amazing general contractor, Pete Playdon. Pete, built like Paul Bunyan and meticulous about cleanliness, ensured everything was in perfect order. His expertise and efficiency made my life much easier as he oversaw the entire process, even though he didn't do all the work himself. Goodness, educators have a lot to learn from general contractors!

I liken the process of designing and facilitating a strong lesson to my renovation project with Pete. Both processes begin with setting clear goals and maintaining a vision of success. Pete, armed with the blueprint, is akin to a teacher equipped with quality instructional materials or a universally designed lesson plan. Much like teachers, Pete and his team had to continuously adapt based on real-time situations and emerging challenges. For instance, when old tiles were removed, unexpected cracks appeared in an adjacent wall, and rerouting plumbing for my longed-for soaking tub damaged some new tiles. Pete navigated these challenges each time, ensuring the work remained high quality.

Teachers are the general contractors of the classroom; we design lessons while distributing the cognitive load, decision-making, and active learning among our students. Teachers must oversee progress, adjust plans, and ensure everyone works toward the shared vision, like Pete. This analogy underscores that while a well-designed plan is crucial, the real magic in teaching lies in its execution—the human connection and responsiveness involved in adaptability, differentiating instruction, providing feedback, and supporting subcontractors and students to deepen their expertise. We must remember that in education, as in construction, a blueprint for implementing UDL or blended learning is just the beginning.

Keyword Alert!

High-quality instructional materials (HQIM): Educational resources (e.g., textbooks, digital content, lesson plans, assessments) designed to support effective teaching and learning. These materials are comprehensive and standards-aligned, and they promote equity and inclusion by providing all students with access to rigorous content.

Catlin and I have worked with countless clients who have asked us to provide professional learning and sample lessons to teachers so they can easily implement UDL and blended learning. We often receive requests for "something teachers can do right away" or "two to three strategies they can use tomorrow." Of course, we can provide lessons and strategies, but we cannot ensure teachers' success given the ever-changing landscape of education and the dynamic and evolving needs of individual learners.

We both have heard this countless times: "I tried UDL or blended learning, but it didn't work." We want to challenge the mindset that a strategy has to work the first time with no adjustments to be considered successful. The true brilliance of teachers is our ability to think critically, adapt based on data, and provide real-time scaffolding to learners, but many of us still struggle to shift our mindsets to prioritize the importance of educational design work.

High-quality instructional materials, educational consultants, and artificial intelligence have the potential to help us generate lesson plans that may look flawless on paper, much like a well-designed blueprint. However, the real effectiveness of such lessons hinges on how they are delivered in the classroom—with a human touch. Simply put, while high-quality instructional materials and sample lessons can lay a strong foundation for learning, a teacher's skill in adapting and delivering these lessons in a responsive and dynamic manner drives student learning and engagement.

Just as I envisioned what I wanted my perfect bathroom to look like, we want to share our vision for what an adaptive teaching practice—one informed by UDL and blended learning principles—can ultimately look like on the ground. In table 2.1, we share the shifts necessary to transition from a high-quality lesson to a universally designed blended lesson.

You may examine the lesson transformation below and think, *No way—that is way too much work.* We argue that it is *not* more work, but rather it is *different* work that requires the adaptive change necessary for student success.

Table 2.1: Adaptive Change for UDL, Blended Learning, and Shift to Student-Led Learning

	Before Adaptive Change	Necessary Shift
Roles	Teachers are seen as the primary source of knowledge, and they direct the learning.	Teachers are facilitators who guide and support students' learning through inquiry, exploration, and collaboration.
Relationships	Teacher-student relationships are often hierarchical, with the teacher directing the flow of information.	Students and teachers are partners in the learning process, working together to discover and make meaning.
Values	Emphasis is typically on uniform teaching methods to transfer information and standardized assessments to evaluate progress toward learning objectives.	We value meaningful choice with a focus on firm goals and flexibility in methods, materials, and assessments.
Behaviors	Teacher behavior often revolves around lecturing, delivering content, and leading all parts of the learning experiences.	Teachers use backward design and blended learning models to universally design lessons, engage with students during instruction, and adopt a responsive teaching style that adapts to students' data, feedback, and needs.
Approaches to the Work	Teachers focus on delivering a set curriculum with a one-size-fits-all approach.	Teachers focus on implementing a flexible approach to curriculum design and delivery that accommodates students' varying paces and learning paths.

Strong Pedagogical Practices

Making adaptive change

Shifting teachers' mindsets about their roles as co-designers and facilitators of instruction is an adaptive challenge, but it is often treated as a technical problem. Technical problems are simple to identify, and they lend themselves to quick solutions. For example, if a school does not have high-quality instructional materials, this can be solved by adopting a new curriculum or shifting to a new unit design process. If there isn't enough time for teachers to collaborate, schools can explore and adopt new schedules. People are often receptive to technical solutions, and as a result they are easy to implement.

Sometimes, though, we don't just need solutions—we need a change. Adaptive work is required when deeply held beliefs are challenged, when the values that made us successful become less relevant, and when legitimate yet competing perspectives emerge. In their seminal article "The Work of Leadership" in the *Harvard Business Review*, Ronald Heifetz and Donald L. Laurie note that adaptive change often challenges employees. They offer, "Adaptive change is distressing for the people going through it. They need to take on new roles, new relationships, new values, new behaviors, and new approaches to work."[1]

Keyword Alert!

Adaptive change: A type of change that requires organizations to learn new ways to do their work or conduct business and to shift their underlying values, behaviors, and mindsets. Adaptive change challenges employees because it goes beyond technical adjustments and involves addressing core beliefs and habits that may no longer be effective in the current environment.

UDL, blended learning, and advances in artificial intelligence require that teachers make adaptive shifts. Let's take a minute to examine a high-quality lesson and reimagine the same lesson through the lens of UDL and blended learning. Then, we will discuss the shifts necessary in teacher roles, relationships, values, behaviors, and approaches to the work. By reimagining a high-quality lesson, we will highlight how to better meet diverse learner needs, leverage technology for personalized learning, and support necessary shifts in teaching roles, relationships, values, and behaviors to effectively support all students.

Root & STEM is a Canadian-based magazine in print and online formats, offering STEAM resources for K–12 educators, particularly for teaching digital skills. Each magazine issue includes culturally responsive lesson plans to foster innovation and creativity. In one lesson, designed by Ayesha Akhlaq,[2] students translate literature to code by reading the poem "Holding Grief" by Ashley Qilavaq-Savard. They discuss the poem, and then they use DALL-E 2 to create an AI-generated rendition of the poem based on their critical analysis. The lesson provides an incredibly strong foundation for learning; it uses high-quality literature by an Indigenous author, empowers students to participate in a community circle, and develops their ability to use advanced digital tools creatively. As with many high-quality instructional materials, numerous areas of the lesson are open to teacher interpretation. By examining these components through the lens of UDL and blended learning, we can further enhance accessibility, engagement, and effectiveness for all students.

The lesson starts with clear instructions: "To begin the lesson, read the poem 'Holding Grief.'" In a more traditional classroom, the teacher may read the poem aloud or ask students to read it silently. The lesson doesn't detail how students access the poem, so that is an example of where teachers can shift responsibility to students. You could ask your students, "Would you rather read a hard copy, access the poem digitally for a read aloud or translation, or work in a small group and have a partner read?" This shift honors the integrity of the lesson and provides students with autonomy and options to become more engaged in their learning.

After reading the poem, the next step is for teachers to lead the discussion with prompts like these:

- In your opinion, what is the format and structure of the poem?
- Determine the voice and tone of the poem. What words or images convey the tone?
- Are you able to decipher the poet's feelings through her words? What do they convey?

Now, both of us can imagine a scenario where a class of students doesn't have strong background knowledge in poetic form or lacks a vocabulary for it, making it challenging to answer a question about the author's word choice. This would require an adaptation of the lesson to provide background knowledge and explicit vocabulary instruction.

In such situations, it's common for some educators to view the lesson as inappropriate or overly challenging for their classes. However, the key is not to simplify the lesson or to lower the standards but to consider the necessary adaptations and scaffolds. This is where a blended learning model can be particularly effective. With blended learning, teachers could develop a playlist of activities that allow their students to enjoy more control over the pace and path of their learning while still accomplishing all the lesson objectives. For instance, the playlist might include these elements:

Figure 2.1: Poetry Lesson Playlist

Poetry Lesson Playlist	
Path	**Student Work**
Review Poetic Vocabulary and Form • Use this link to explore our poetry vocabulary and form choice board. • Select as many items from the board as necessary to prepare for the quiz that allows you to move forward in the playlist. If you do not pass the quiz, you'll need to return to the choice board to do more review. Option: You can work alone or work with a partner on this choice board review activity.	Capture your notes here or on paper. You can list terms with definitions or create a visual representation of what you learned.
Quiz: Time to Check Your Understanding • Use your notes to complete this quiz to check your understanding of key poetry vocabulary and common forms used in poetry. You are welcome to use your notes! • If you pass the quiz, you may move on to the next activity. If you did not pass, please spend more time on the choice board review and try the quiz again.	Step 1: Capture your scores here for each attempt. Step 2: Complete the "I used to think, now, I think..." thinking routine to reflect on how the review impacted your thinking about poetry.
Read "Holding Grief" by Ashley Qilavaq-Savard • Decide how you want to read the poem, and as you read, pay close attention to the words used. Poems are short, so every word matters! Option: You can read a paper copy of the poem, access it online for translation aids, or listen to an audio version I created for you.	Underline or circle interesting or important words if you are reading on paper or make a list below if you are reading online or listening to the audio version.
Teacher Check-in: Let's Chat about the Poem	
Online Discussion Participation • Respond to the discussion questions, sharing your thoughts on the poem and brainstorming your ideas in response to the questions. Option: You can respond via text (LMS) or video (Flip).	

As students work through this poetry playlist, they benefit from a high degree of control over the pace at which they work and the path *through* which they work. This is because they can make key decisions throughout the process. Since the playlist is essentially a one-stop resource shop, the teacher is free to use their time strategically. For example, as most students begin the first step of the playlist, the teacher can pull individual learners or small groups for more scaffolded instruction and review, differentiating and personalizing support. Students who speak English as a second language may need more teacher support to build the poetic vocabulary necessary to complete the lesson. Students with little to no background knowledge of poetic form will benefit from targeted instruction on the specific forms they will encounter in this and future lessons.

We also encourage you to include teacher check-ins on your playlists to ensure all students get small-group or individual time with you. In our example, once students have completed the reading portion of the playlist, the teacher check-in can be used to collect formative assessment data, which will allow you to check for understanding. This time can be used to discuss the poem, the author's word choice, tone, format, etc., so you can help students deepen their understanding of the poem and address any gaps or misconceptions they may have after their initial reading. This dedicated time in class to work with individuals and small groups can boost students' confidence in their reading and comprehension skills and develop your relationships with learners.

Utilizing a blended learning approach and incorporating UDL will give students more control over their learning experience and proactively remove barriers. In this way, you can support all students in engaging with and understanding the complex material presented in a high-quality lesson. However, even with these changes, students may struggle at a step in the playlist and require further adaptations and support. That's why it is critical for you to maximize your time as students work and prioritize individual interactions.

The Danielson Framework

The Danielson Framework for Teaching (FFT), developed by Charlotte Danielson, is a foundational instructional framework, particularly in the United States, where it has significantly shaped educational practices.[3] The FFT addresses the challenge of ensuring high-quality, consistent instructional practices across diverse educational settings and offers a structured solution to improve teaching effectiveness and student outcomes by providing clear expectations and guidance for educators. The framework's emphasis on adaptable and responsive instruction is particularly relevant. The FFT consists of four domains: planning and preparation, learning environments, learning experiences, and principled teaching. Each domain represents a broad area of teaching practice that includes specific components and elements of effective instruction. We want to summarize each domain and note the importance of consistently adapting instruction to meet the needs of learners.

Domain 1: Planning and Preparation. The planning and preparation domain describes how teachers organize instruction for student learning. We love how Danielson introduces this domain with the following explanation. "It is difficult to overstate the importance of planning and preparation. One could argue that a teacher's role is not so much to teach as it is to arrange for learning." As described in our earlier anecdote about Katie's bathroom, Pete didn't renovate as much as he arranged for the bathroom renovation through careful planning and preparation. Because the lesson-planning process entails identifying firm goals, considering how to make high-quality instructional materials that meet the needs of diverse students, and adapting instruction based on formative assessment data, this domain means embracing the ideals of UDL and blended learning.

Domain 2: Learning Environments. This domain describes the conditions and qualities of environments that are conducive to learning and supporting student success. This includes fostering a culture of learning, maintaining purposeful environments, supporting positive student behavior, and organizing spaces for learning.

As with Domain 1, Domain 2 mirrors UDL's principle of providing multiple means of engagement and honoring student voice and choice to create purposeful, motivating learning environments where students consistently contribute to the design and delivery of instruction, make responsible decisions about their learning, and reflect on their progress toward firm goals. Universally designed learning environments are not the passive lecture halls of the past. Rather, they are active learning spaces where students can communicate, collaborate, and apply their learning.

Similarly, blended learning strives to position students as active agents in the learning process through an intentional combination of online and offline learning. The goal of blended learning is to shift control over key aspects of the learning experience and environment to students, specifically the elements of time, place, pace, and path. If you're thinking, *Wait, control over the place? They are in my classroom*, we are even talking about how you strategically use the spaces in your classroom. Can we invite students to use those spaces (e.g., reading corner, tables grouped together for collaboration) effectively to engage in different types of learning experiences? In a blended learning environment, shifting control to students is at the heart of the rotation models. As a result, students must assume more responsibility for managing their behavior, directing their learning, advocating for their specific needs, and engaging with their peers to construct knowledge.

Domain 3: Learning Experiences. This domain focuses on engaging students in inclusive learning experiences that enhance student achievement and growth. Strong pedagogical practices to achieve this include communicating the purpose of learning experiences, using questioning and discussion techniques that foster deep learning, engaging students cognitively and socially, and responding flexibly to student needs (yippee!).

Domain 3 clarifies that creating learning experiences is equally the responsibility of students and teachers. Working collaboratively toward that goal requires providing opportunities for students to make decisions about their learning, reflect on those decisions, and receive feedback to help them learn and grow. This also means teachers need to adapt instruction and feedback based on student data. Incorporating that feedback in a lockstep, whole-class environment is impossible. Instead, blended learning models, like playlists and station rotation, provide opportunities for peer feedback, small-group differentiated instruction, small-group student-led discussions, side-by-side assessment, and personalized real-time feedback sessions.

Domain 4: Principled Teaching. Domain 4 is the work educators do that extends beyond their classrooms and the learning experiences they facilitate (note that word *facilitate* again). This encompasses the teacher engaging in reflective practice, documenting student progress, engaging families and communities, contributing to school community and culture, growing and developing professionally, and acting in service of students.

Domain 4 is where change happens. As educators, our role is to continually reflect and adapt to meet the beautifully diverse needs of the students we serve. We know, without a doubt, that educators want students to be successful, but many of them aren't *yet*. We cannot hold on to practices of the past that no longer serve our students or prepare them for the world ahead. As we reflect on our current practices, their impact on the students and families we serve, and our responsibility to continually learn and grow, we must be aware of the barriers we create if we have negative mindsets about change.

We know, without a doubt, that educators want students to be successful, but many of them aren't yet. We cannot hold on to practices of the past that no longer serve our students or prepare them for the world ahead. As we reflect on our current practices, their impact on the students and families we serve, and our responsibility to continually learn and grow, we must be aware of the barriers we create if we have negative mindsets about change.

Yes, teaching may be easier if students sit like sweet little glazed donuts while we deliver a one-size-fits-all lesson, but this is not how our students have evolved, so we must adapt our practice—despite the discomfort. None of us signed up for this work because it was easy; we signed up to inspire students and help them become life-long learners.

The most impactful educators recognize that their journey is one of continuous growth and learning—right alongside their students. They engage in reflective practice rooted in their interactions with students, constantly seeking feedback that provides them with opportunities to adapt and improve their teaching strategies to ensure accessibility, engagement, and positive outcomes for *every* learner.

Leveraging AI

Change is hard, and many educators struggle with it. Let's be honest: most people do, regardless of their profession! Two Harvard

Graduate School of Education faculty members—Robert Kegan and Lisa Lahey—have built a body of research to help adult learners overcome their aversion to adaptive change, a phenomenon Kegan and Lahey call immunity to change.[4] Immunity to change is a five-step process.

1. Commit to a change goal.
2. Describe the behavior you need to change.
3. Uncover your hidden competing commitments.
4. Tease out your big assumptions.
5. Test your assumptions.

Let's examine what this may look like when a teacher more familiar with one-size-fits-all instruction is asked to adapt to UDL and blended learning while figuring out how to manage and use emerging technology (Table 2.2).

Table 2.2: Immunity to Change in UDL and Blended Learning

Step	Educator Response
Commit to a Change Goal	I want to design flexible, universally designed lessons so students are engaged and learn at high levels while becoming more engaged and self-directed in their learning.
Behavior That Needs to Change	I need to adopt backward design and blended learning models for lesson planning, actively engage with students during instruction, and employ a responsive teaching style that adapts to students' data, feedback, and needs.
Competing Commitments	• I am hesitant to spend excessive time designing lessons due to a lack of time and existing overwhelming responsibilities. • I am concerned that new approaches might not yield positive outcomes, impacting my confidence in my professional abilities. • I value maintaining control in my classroom to ensure effectiveness and student learning.

Big Assumptions	• Spending more time designing lessons will only increase my workload and further overwhelm me. • Experimenting with new teaching methods could result in poorer outcomes, negatively reflecting my teaching skills. • A controlled classroom environment is essential for effective teaching and learning.
Test Your Assumptions	• To challenge the assumption about increased workload, start by implementing new planning strategies in small, manageable segments using AI tools. For example, redesign one lesson per week using backward design and blended learning models, and monitor the time spent on this task during your prep period or PLC meeting versus its impact on student engagement and learning. • Document student feedback and learning outcomes after implementing these changes to address the fear of worse outcomes. Compare these with previous methods to objectively assess student performance and engagement differences. • Test the assumption regarding control by gradually introducing more student-led activities and observing the effects on classroom dynamics and student learning. • Reflect on how this shift impacts both your teaching experience and student outcomes. If you need support, contact an instructional coach, a trusted colleague, or an administrator to give feedback on potential shifts.

Too often, professional learning addresses how to change behavior without addressing why people are resistant to the change in the first place. To implement adaptive change, we must openly discuss our competing commitments and the underlying assumptions we hold about change, even though this can be challenging. Acknowledging and confronting our fears and assumptions about change is critical. To better meet the needs of our learners, we must be clear about our outcomes, universally design lessons, leverage blended learning, and use data to adapt and differentiate instruction and support. These are not just tasks to be checked off a to-do list; they are strong pedagogical practices imperative for student success.

Change is hard but necessary. AI can be a great thought partner to help you test your assumptions and take the next steps in your journey toward implementing UDL and blended learning. We have reimagined the immunity-to-change process in terms of lesson planning with AI. This chapter's engagement with AI will be a bit more involved than it will be later in the book (when we shift toward prompts that you can employ for your own purposes). However, by exploring our time with ChatGPT at length, we hope to model how you can position AI as a powerful thought partner.

Identify Improvement Goals

Determine what you want to change in the existing lesson. For instance, the goal could be to incorporate elements of UDL and blended learning to increase active learning and student agency. You could also focus on one of the pedagogical practices from the Danielson Framework. For our purposes today, though, let's return to the poetry lesson we examined earlier and give it a UDL- and blended-learning-infused renovation! Along the way, let's incorporate the immunity-to-change steps outlined above.

> **Catlin and Katie:** We have a lesson where students translate literature to code by reading the poem "Holding Grief" by Ashley Qilavaq-Savard. They discuss the poem and then use DALL-E 2 to create an AI-generated rendition of the poem based on their critical analysis. Please revise the lesson with UDL and blended learning to give students more opportunities to demonstrate agency.

> **ChatGPT:** To revise the lesson on translating the poem "Holding Grief" by Ashley Qilavaq-Savard into code with a focus on UDL and Blended Learning consider the following strategies:

1. Pre-Lesson Activities for Background Knowledge and Engagement:
   - Create a playlist of short videos, articles, and interactive materials on poetic forms, coding basics, and the intersection of literature and technology. This caters to diverse learning preferences and builds foundational knowledge.
   - Use a learning management system where students can access these resources at their own pace and choose the ones that resonate with them, increasing engagement and self-directed learning.
2. Reading and Accessing the Poem:
   - Provide the poem in various formats—printed copies, digital text with annotation tools, and an audio version. This ensures accessibility for all learners, including those with specific learning needs. Allow students to select their preferred format to engage with the poem, fostering autonomy and catering to individual learning preferences.
3. Discussion and Analysis:
   - Utilize tools like discussion forums or collaborative documents where students can post their initial thoughts, questions, and interpretations of the poem. This can include text, audio, or video responses.
   - Encourage interactive feedback where both the teacher and peers can respond, offering diverse perspectives and deepening understanding.
4. Translating Literature to Code:
   - Students apply their understanding of the poem and coding skills to create an AI-generated rendition using DALL-E 2. They work on this project in stages in a playlist, receiving ongoing feedback.
5. Presentation and Reflection:
   - Allow students to present their AI-generated renditions in a class gallery, either virtually or in the classroom. This can include a short explanation of their interpretation and coding process.
   - Encourage students to maintain a reflective journal throughout the project, documenting their learning

process, challenges, and insights. This can be done digitally or in a traditional notebook.

Identify Competing Commitments

Catlin and Katie: I am concerned this will take me too much time to plan, especially to curate all the resources in step 1. Is there a way to make this process more efficient and shift to student-led?

ChatGPT: An efficient and engaging idea to shift to student-led is to organize a collaborative resource-gathering activity. Here's how you can structure it:

1. Group Formation: Divide the class into small groups. Each group will have a specific aspect of poetry to research and present to the class. These aspects could include poetic forms, elements of poetry (like metaphors, similes, rhythm, etc.), or different cultures' poetic traditions.
2. Research Assignment: Assign each group a specific online platform or resource to explore. For example, one group could use the Poetry Foundation website, another could explore the Academy of American Poets' resources, and others could look at different educational poetry websites or digital libraries.
3. Collaborative Learning: Encourage groups to collaborate on finding resources relevant to their assigned aspect of poetry. They can use tools like shared digital documents or online boards (like Google Docs or Padlet) to compile and annotate their findings. This activity enhances research skills and fosters teamwork.
4. Individual Exploration: Finally, give students time to individually explore the resources gathered by their peers. They can use these insights to enhance their understanding of the poem and to inform their coding project.

This activity not only makes the lesson planning more efficient and student-led but also enriches the learning experience by incorporating diverse perspectives and resources. It actively engages students in the learning process and encourages them to take ownership of their education.

Other prompts you could try to identify competing commitments with AI are:

- "One concern I have about adapting this lesson with UDL and blended learning elements is . . ."
- "What small steps can I take to start integrating UDL and blended learning into my teaching without feeling overwhelmed?"

Test Assumptions

Catlin and Katie: What evidence can I collect to see if these UDL and blended learning changes are positively impacting student engagement and learning outcomes?

ChatGPT: To gauge the impact of the changes you've implemented in your classroom, you can collect various forms of evidence to assess student engagement and learning outcomes. Here are some effective methods:

- Student Surveys and Feedback: Use surveys or questionnaires to gather students' perceptions about the changes in teaching methods. Ask specific questions about their level of engagement, understanding, and interest in the lesson content.
- Observation Notes: Regularly jot down observational notes during lessons. These notes can capture student behaviors that indicate engagement, such as participation in

discussions, active involvement in group work, and focused attention during activities.
- Performance Data: Analyze grades and performance data from quizzes, tests, or other formal assessments. Look for trends or changes in student performance that might correlate with the instructional changes you've implemented.
- Reflection Journals: If students maintain learning journals or reflection logs, review these for insights into their thoughts and feelings about the learning process, as well as their self-assessed understanding of the material.

In the section above, ChatGPT's suggestions provide a framework for assessing the impact of UDL and blended learning changes on student engagement and learning outcomes. Together, these methods create a comprehensive evidence base, helping educators objectively evaluate the effectiveness of their instructional changes and make informed adjustments as needed to improve the outcomes of all learners.

To further enhance the integration of UDL and blended learning into your lessons and to utilize AI as a scaffold and support, it's important to align these practices with the Danielson Framework's considerations for flexible, adaptive lessons. Once you generate a lesson with AI and create a strong blueprint for instruction, reflect on the following questions, adapted from the Danielson Framework:

- How do the instructional outcomes in the lesson align with grade-level standards to ensure ambitious instruction for all students?
- Does the lesson include formative assessments that will allow for adjustments to instruction to support student agency?
- During the lesson, how will I apply student input to create a sense of shared ownership?
- Where in the lesson will students monitor their own understanding to analyze their progress toward learning goals?

- When in the lesson will students receive and engage with high-quality feedback to enhance their learning?

Using these self-assessment questions as you transition to more UDL lessons using blended learning models ensures that you are not only implementing strong pedagogical practices but also fostering a growth-oriented mindset. This mindset is key to embracing the dynamic, flexible nature of education, adapting to diverse learner needs, and fostering an environment where both students and educators can continuously develop and thrive. By reflecting on these questions, you can cultivate a mindset that values adaptability, innovation, and responsive teaching, which are essential in the effective application of UDL and blended learning.

One-Sentence Summary

Adaptive teaching through UDL and blended learning requires educators to embrace change, utilize AI as a supportive tool, and continuously reflect on their practices to enhance student engagement and learning outcomes.

Reflect and Discuss

1. Consider the parallels between a general contractor's work and educational facilitation. How can you, as an educator, incorporate project management and adaptability into your teaching practice?

2. Reflect on your own immunity to change when it comes to adopting UDL and blended learning strategies in your classroom. What competing commitments or underlying assumptions are holding you back from fully embracing these methods?

3. How are you currently implementing UDL and blended learning in your classroom? Reflect on specific examples or strategies you

have used. What successes and challenges have you encountered in integrating these approaches into your teaching practice?

4. Consider the Danielson Framework for Teaching. How do you ensure that UDL and blended learning consistently align with strong pedagogical practices, as outlined in this framework? Reflect on how this alignment enhances your teaching effectiveness and supports student learning outcomes.

Time to Apply!

1. Revisit the goal you set for yourself at the end of chapter 1.
2. Use the immunity-to-change model to do the following:
   a) Identify your current behaviors that need to change for you to achieve this goal.
   b) List your competing commitments that are causing your current behaviors.
   c) List your big assumptions.
   d) Consider how you will test your assumptions.
3. Complete the table below as you work through the process.

Step	Your Response
Commit to a Change Goal	
Behavior That Needs to Change	
Competing Commitments	
Big Assumptions	
Test Your Assumptions	

PART I

Establishing a Foundation

Design Path

STEP 1
Identify Desired Results
Align Desired Results and Assessment Strategy

CHAPTER 3

Identify Desired Results

Cross-Country College Quest

Catlin "I think I might want to apply to some Ivy League colleges, Mom!" My daughter Cheyenne made this proclamation in the fall of her junior year. For years, she had talked about applying exclusively to schools in California, where we live. So, I was shocked that my daughter, who is a bit of a homebody and a definite mama's girl, would be interested in applying to schools all the way across the country. She is an impressive student—highly motivated and academically successful—so being accepted by an elite East Coast university is definitely within the realm of possibility. Despite knowing she's capable of the academic rigor of such a college, the mom in me began to think about all the factors she would need to consider before even beginning the application process. Does the school offer majors in the subjects she is most interested in? What is the faculty-to-student ratio? Could my little California girl really handle months of cold weather?

These were not questions I could answer for my daughter. And without seeing the colleges that interested her in person, she could not make an informed decision either. So, I proposed a mommy-daughter trip to the East Coast, but I told Cheyenne I also wanted her to participate in planning the trip.

In our initial conversation, I asked Cheyenne, "What would make our trip feel like a success for you?" I wanted clarity on the desired results of this trip before we embarked on the planning process. She was quick to respond that she wanted to "get a feel" for each college and the surrounding area to see if she could imagine living there for four years. Since she had only been on a couple college campuses, she wanted to get a better idea of how she would evaluate colleges and decide if they were a good fit and worth applying to. Second, she wanted to enjoy quality time together! With those objectives in mind, I asked her to research colleges and identify five schools to visit and tour. She spent a month researching schools and was able to eliminate a few based on factors like location.

Once Cheyenne had decided on the schools she wanted to visit, I asked her to create an itinerary. After she had completed her proposed schedule (as a Google Slides deck, no less!) with the locations of each campus, driving directions to and from each, and the tour information and time, I got to work on the travel details. Since one main goal of our week was to enjoy intensive mommy-daughter bonding time, I knew renting a car would be better than using ride-sharing apps or catching trains. In our own car, we could blast the "This Is Taylor Swift" Spotify channel and enjoy snacks and stop for Starbucks along the way. I also booked a room near each campus so we could walk around and explore the surrounding neighborhoods.

As we put the finishing touches on our trip, I asked Cheyenne to think about how she would evaluate each college and capture her impressions. I said I'd love for her to list all the factors she thought were important to consider. That way, we could discuss them in the car or over dinner each night. I hoped that those conversations and her documentation of the experience would clarify which colleges she wanted to apply to.

This approach mirrors the backward design process in education, where identifying desired results is followed by determining an assessment strategy. We planned the college trip by focusing on the outcome Cheyenne wanted—to get a feel for the schools and to spend quality time together—and then created a strategy to evaluate each school. Teachers should begin their design work by identifying the desired results for a unit of study and then develop an assessment strategy to measure student progress toward those results. By starting with clear goals and defining how success will be measured, teachers can create cohesive units that effectively guide students toward achieving those outcomes.

Teachers often find themselves overwhelmed and frustrated when they dive into lesson planning without a clear vision of the desired outcomes. This common pitfall results in a fragmented approach where activities and assessments may not align with the essential learning goals. The result? Units may feel disjointed, students struggle to see the relevance of their work, and teachers must constantly adjust their plans on the fly. If you don't start with the end in mind, it's easy to get lost in the details and miss the big picture, leading to missed opportunities for deep, meaningful learning.

Backward design encourages teachers to first identify and articulate the desired results and then plan backward to ensure every lesson, activity, and assessment aligns with those goals. This approach provides a clear road map for instruction, resulting in more coherence, focus, and depth.

Strong Pedagogical Practices

Backward Design: Beginning with the End in Mind

When we plan for desired results, we embrace the philosophy of backward design. As discussed in chapter 1, backward design refocuses our approach to designing learning experiences by emphasizing outcomes rather than the subject matter, course materials, or particular teaching techniques. This approach entails prioritizing what students should learn over how we traditionally teach the topic.

To review, here are the three steps in backward design:

1. Articulate desired results or the destination that you and your students need to work toward.
2. Decide on an assessment strategy that will help you measure student progress toward the desired result.
3. Design a learning path to guide all students students toward the desired result.

This chapter will explore how teachers can take the first step using their subject and grade-level standards and AI as a design partner. In the next chapter, we'll discuss step 2 in detail. We'll cover step 3 throughout part II, diving into the work of designing equitable lessons and learning experiences.

Distinguishing Standards from Desired Results and Learning Objectives

Education is full of words that get used interchangeably, but we want to be clear about what we mean by the terms *educational standards*, *desired results*, and *learning objectives*—while having a little fun!

We love getting lost in a good book by a cozy fire with a hot cup of coffee. So, let's reimagine education standards, desired results, and learning objectives through the lens of a universally beloved story: "Cinderella." Just like genre sets the tone and expectations for an author working on a book, standards outline the educational journey ahead, providing a framework for what students should learn at each grade level and in each subject area. However, just as a genre doesn't require specific characters, settings, themes, or plot details, standards do not dictate exactly how a teacher should teach a concept or help students apply a skill. They do not suggest specific instructional models or teaching strategies, and many do not designate specific texts or resources. Instead, the creative work of designing learning experiences to meet standards is left up to educators and curriculum designers. Similarly, the author enjoys the creative license to interpret and apply the genre norms and the corresponding literary tropes in their own way to create a captivating story that will appeal to readers.

> **Keyword Alert!**
>
> **Educational standards:** The learning goals and benchmarks established by educational authorities that outline what students should know and be able to do at each grade level. These standards serve as a framework for curriculum development, instructional practices, and assessments, ensuring consistency and accountability in education across different schools and districts.

Desired results are akin to the impact an author wants to have on the reader. For "Cinderella," the universal themes of resilience, hope, and transformation inspire readers across cultures. In education, students emerge with a deep understanding of a particular concept, the confidence to apply specific skills in a variety of contexts, and, hopefully, a better sense of themselves as learners.

> **Keyword Alert!**
>
> **Desired results:** Specific outcomes that educators aim to achieve within the framework of educational standards. Desired results translate the general expectations outlined by standards into concrete, measurable objectives that guide day-to-day teaching and learning activities.

To extend the story analogy, the individual learning objectives within a unit are like the key moments in "Cinderella." These objectives guide the daily activities and lessons, paralleling each pivotal event in the story, bringing readers deeper into the narrative, moving them closer to the resolution. Just as Cinderella's experiences unfold to reveal her character's depth and resilience (she faces challenges with her stepmother and stepsisters, and she eventually triumphs when the glass slipper fits!), lesson objectives unfold, propelling students toward a unit's ultimate desired result. But, as we will explore in the next chapter, there are lots of ways that students might meet each lesson objective on their journey to the desired result.

Keyword Alert!

Learning objectives: Detailed, actionable goals for individual lessons and activities that break down desired results into a series of smaller learning goals. This alignment ensures that instructional practices are focused on helping students meet or exceed the established standards, providing a clear and coherent path for academic success.

Many teachers, departments, teaching teams, and curriculum designers begin their design work with grade-level, subject-area standards. Standards identify what students should know and be able to do at the end of each school year in each subject. Importantly, though, as Sarah Schwartz reminds us, "Standards are not a curriculum, though. They don't outline the day-to-day lessons and activities teachers use; rather, they provide an end goal for instruction."[1] In other words, while standards set the target, it is up to educators to create specific lessons and activities that will help students reach those goals.

Standards are a guide to help educators and curriculum designers identify the core concepts and skills students need to learn in each subject at each grade level. However, Wiggins and McTighe (2005)[2] make the point that most standards are so jam-packed with concepts and skills that teachers and curriculum designers need to spend time and energy untangling standards to understand what they want to prioritize—since there is rarely enough time to cover it all. Districts and schools that prioritize standards help make teachers' work more manageable by allowing us the space to design lessons that focus on depth, not breadth. When we feel pressure to cover *every* aspect of *every* standard, we end up racing through content and skills with a coverage mentality instead of allowing students the time and space to engage deeply with subject-area concepts and spend time applying skills with teacher and peer support.

Some may treat standards as though they are synonymous with desired results, but we want to make a clear distinction between the two, as shown in table 3.1.

Table 3.1: Standards Versus Desired Result

Subject-Area Standards	Desired Result of a Unit
Standards are overarching goals that articulate what students should know and be able to do, often over the course of a school year or a specific grade level. Standards provide a framework or a set of benchmarks for what students should achieve.	While standards provide the overarching goals applicable across multiple units and often across grade levels, the desired results of a specific unit are tailored to the topic and content of that unit. The desired result considers the unique focus, materials, and themes of the unit. It addresses specific content, skills, or understandings that are relevant in the context of that unit.
Example: One of the National Core Art Anchor Standards requires students to synthesize and relate knowledge and personal experiences to make art.	**Example:** While working toward the standard "synthesize and relate knowledge and personal experiences to make art" in a ceramics class, the desired results may be: Integrate and apply knowledge of various ceramics techniques, historical art movements, and the properties of clay to produce a unique piece that incorporates elements from life experiences, demonstrating the ability to connect personal history, emotions, and perspectives with artistic expression.

Exploring specific standards can serve as a useful exercise in deducing desired results and working toward individual lesson objectives. So, let's look at a third-grade Next Generation Science Standard (NGSS) focused on ecosystems, as well as a ninth-grade Common Core ELA Reading Literature Standard, shown in table 3.2.

Table 3.2: Examples of Standards, Desired Results, and Lesson Objectives

	Third-Grade Science	Ninth-Grade English Language Arts
The Standard	3-LS2-1 Construct an argument that some animals form groups that help members survive.	RL.9-10.2 Determine a theme or central idea of a text and analyze in detail its development over the course of the text, including how it emerges and is shaped and refined by specific details; provide an objective summary of the text.
Desired Result	• By the conclusion of our exploration into the rainforest ecosystem, students will be able to explain why some rainforest animals team up to stay safe and find food. They will use what they have learned to make a strong argument, showing how working together helps animals survive in the rainforest. • Students will research a specific animal group behavior and demonstrate their understanding by creating an artifact that illustrates how this behavior contributes to the survival and well-being of the group.	• By the end of our unit on empathy, students will be able to identify and analyze the central themes in short stories and the novel *To Kill a Mockingbird*. • Students will examine how a central theme emerges in the text and analyze its development through the narrative, focusing on specific details such as character actions, setting, and symbolism.

| Lesson Objectives | • Students will understand what the rainforest ecosystem is and how it is unique from other ecosystems.
• Students will be able to list common animal groups in the rainforest (such as herds, flocks, and packs) and the unique behaviors of each type of animal group.
• Students will identify and explain the advantages of living in groups for animals, such as increased protection from predators or improved hunting efficiency.
• Each student will select one animal species in the rainforest that exhibits a specific group behavior and conduct research to understand the nature and benefits of this behavior.
• Students will learn how to construct a basic argument. | • Students will learn what the word *theme* means and practice reading short stories to identify and articulate the central theme.
• Students will read "Tuesday Siesta" by Gabriel García Márquez and identify the theme of the short story. They will practice analyzing (with teacher guidance) how the elements of a narrative, such as characters, setting, plot, and symbolism, help an author develop a theme.
• Students will read "Marigolds" by Eugenia Collier and discuss their initial impressions of the story. They will brainstorm potential themes and how these themes might relate to their own experiences.
• Students will analyze the protagonist, Lizabeth, and other key characters in "Marigolds," focusing on how their actions and transformations contribute to developing the story's themes.
• Students will explore the setting of "Marigolds" and discuss its significance to the story's themes. They will also examine the symbolism of the marigolds and how they represent various aspects of the themes.
• Students will apply what they learned reading a collection of short stories to the novel *To Kill a Mockingbird*, focusing on how Harper Lee uses characters, setting, and symbolism to develop themes in the novel. |

While these standards serve as important guidelines, they also allow room for interpretation. In the third-grade NGSS science example above, the standard, or performance evidence, makes it clear that students will need to be able to construct an argument about how animals form groups that help members survive. But it does not describe what specific ecosystems or animal groups the students will focus on or how they'll learn about the different animal groups and their behaviors. That is where the more unit-specific desired result can narrow the focus. In this example, the teacher is designing a unit around the rainforest ecosystem. The unit's desired result is more focused and detailed, guiding the students through a process of exploration, conducting research, structuring an argument, and creating an artifact that makes a compelling argument. This is all aimed at building a deeper understanding of the standard's broader concept: the impact of animal group behaviors on survival.

Similarly, the ninth-grade Common Core ELA Reading Literature Standard identifies a specific reading skill (finding a central theme and analyzing its development), but it does not dictate whether a teacher focuses on a collection of short stories or a novel. It does not identify the specific themes students will encounter or how they will learn to analyze thematic development (e.g., in small groups or whole groups). Instead, language like "a text" and "specific details" allows teachers to pull from their materials or curriculum to craft desired results specific to the unit.

AI Integration

Unpacking Standards

Due to the open-ended nature of standards, unpacking them and articulating a student-friendly desired result for a unit may feel daunting. In their book *Understanding by Design*,[3] Wiggins and McTighe identify three major problems educators encounter when using their standards to design their curriculum. First, it is almost impossible to teach students all the concepts and skills included in most standards. As a result, educators must decide which to prioritize in their design work. Second, standards may be too broad or too narrow. When the standard is too broad, knowing what to focus on or how much time to dedicate to it is challenging. Conversely, when the standard is too narrow, it may feel disconnected from larger and more important concepts and skills. The final problem educators face when using standards to inform their design work is that they are often written vaguely, inviting myriad interpretations.

Given these challenges, we want educators to leverage AI as a design partner. It can break down and analyze complex educational standards and help educators identify critical concepts, skills, and competencies that students are expected to develop. AI can also provide examples and resources that align with these components, helping teachers visualize how standards can be applied.

To help educators use AI to unpack their standards, we have crafted a collection of prompts, as shown in table 3.3.

Table 3.3: How AI Can Help Educators Unpack Standards

How AI Can Help Educators Unpack Standards	
Tackling Problem #1: Too Much to Cover	• Can you break down this standard into its key components? What conceptual knowledge and methods or processes are embedded in this standard? • What are the core concepts and essential skills covered in [insert standard]? • Which concepts in these standards are foundational for understanding more complex ideas in [subject]? • Which skills in these standards are foundational for understanding more complex ideas in [subject]? • Can you list this standard's key facts, concepts, and ideas? • In this strand of standards, which concepts and skills are essential and should be prioritized?
Tackling Problem #2: Standards Are Too Broad or Too Narrow	• What are the key concepts in this broad standard? What is essential for students to understand? • What skills in this broad standard should be prioritized? • How can this broad standard be broken down into a sequence of smaller, more manageable learning objectives? • If I have [time frame] to teach this broad standard, which aspects of this standard are most critical for students' understanding of [subject]? • How can I prioritize the content within this standard to ensure depth over breadth of understanding? • How does this narrow standard connect to broader themes or concepts in [subject]? • Why is this narrow standard important within [subject] and/or [grade level]? • How can this standard be presented in a way that highlights its relevance to larger, more comprehensive learning goals? • What real-world applications or examples illustrate the importance of this narrow standard? • How can this standard be taught so that students appreciate its significance? • What strategies can be used to link this narrow standard with other related standards or concepts?

Tackling Problem #3: Unclear or Vague Standards	• What examples or scenarios can illustrate what students should be able to know or do as a result of this standard? • What are the specific skills or knowledge components implicit in this standard that need to be addressed? • What is the underlying intent or educational purpose of this standard? • How does this standard connect to other standards in [grade level/subject area]?

Unpacking standards transforms abstract educational goals into concrete, actionable objectives. This clarity is essential for designing effective units of study that are focused, coherent, and aligned with clear learning outcomes. It ensures that both teaching and learning are purposeful. And when teachers understand the concepts and skills that need to be taught, it makes it much easier to craft a clear desired result for a unit.

Crafting a Desired Result

Think of your desired result as the destination you and your students are heading toward in a unit. It is designed to keep the focus on the learner and make it easier for you to design learning experiences that will help students achieve standards successfully. By crafting a clear statement articulating the learning destination, you are less likely to slip into a coverage mentality, racing through the curriculum without a clear understanding of the larger goals of individual lessons.

If the goal of a unit of study is for a student to apply their learning in a specific way, then desired results allow you to focus your energy on supporting progress toward that goal. A student-friendly desired result can also help learners focus their energy on achieving a specific outcome. So, if students understand the purpose of their work and the unit's goal, it can help them stay engaged in the process and positively impact their self-awareness and self-regulation skills.[4,5]

A strong desired result should meet the following criteria:

- **Specific:** The desired result should clearly state what students are expected to know and be able to do by the end of the unit.
- **Measurable:** The desired result should be something a teacher can observe or quantify since teachers will need to assess progress toward it. Using measurable action verbs is important!
- **Achievable:** The desired result should present a realistic challenge, given the timing and scope of the unit. This is why unpacking the standards to understand what needs to be taught is an essential first step.
- **Relevant:** The desired result should be directly related to key concepts and skills identified in grade-level and subject-area standards, but it should also consider the focus of the unit and the students' interests if we want them to be fully engaged in the learning process.
- **Student-centered:** The language of the desired result should focus on what students will learn and be able to do, not what the teacher will cover.

Investing the time to think through these details and incorporate them into the desired result will create a solid foundation on which to build a cohesive unit.

AI is a wonderful thought partner for teachers or curriculum designers feeling daunted by the prospect of crafting a desired result that incorporates all these attributes! It can support educators in crafting a specific, measurable, achievable, relevant, and student-centered desired result for each unit. When prompted, AI can suggest learning outcomes that align with the unpacked standards, ensuring that each unit is purposefully designed to meet these goals. AI can also help educators put the desired result in student-friendly language so our learners understand what we are working toward.

Let's move through the process of using AI to unpack a first-grade Common Core Math Standard and articulate a desired result for a unit of study.

Catlin and Katie: The first-grade math standard in the operations and algebraic thinking strand reads, "Use addition and subtraction within 20 to solve word problems involving situations of adding to, taking from, putting together, taking apart, and comparing, with unknowns in all positions, e.g., by using objects, drawings, and equations with a symbol for the unknown number to represent the problem." What specific concepts and skills must students learn to meet that standard?

ChatGPT: To meet the first-grade math standard you mentioned, students need to develop a range of skills and understand specific concepts related to addition and subtraction within 20. Here's a breakdown:

1. Understanding of Addition and Subtraction: The foundational concept is understanding what addition and subtraction mean. Addition is combining two or more groups of objects, while subtraction is taking away from a group of objects.
2. Number Sense within 20: Students need to be familiar with numbers up to 20, understanding their sequence and the relationships between these numbers.
3. Solving Word Problems: The ability to interpret simple word problems that describe a real-world situation. This involves identifying whether to add or subtract and what the numbers in the problem represent.
4. Creating and Using Representations: Using objects (like counters or blocks), drawings, or other visual aids to model the problems. This helps students visualize and solve problems more effectively.
5. Formulating Equations: Understanding and creating mathematical equations that correspond to the word

problems. This involves using symbols (like +, −, and =) and can include a symbol (often a question mark or a blank space) for the unknown number.

6. Dealing with Unknowns in Different Positions: Being able to solve problems where the unknown isn't always the result. For example, in the problem "5 + ? = 7", the unknown is the second number in the addition, not the sum.

7. Comparative Reasoning: Understanding and solving problems that involve comparison, such as "How many more?" or "How many fewer?" This requires relating subtraction to comparing quantities.

8. Mental Math and Strategies for Addition and Subtraction: Developing strategies for quick and efficient calculation, like counting on, counting back, making ten, doubles, etc.

9. Fluency with Basic Addition and Subtraction Facts: Building fluency in recalling basic addition and subtraction facts within 20, which aids in solving more complex problems more quickly.

10. Problem-Solving Skills: General skills like reading comprehension (to understand the problem), logical reasoning (to figure out what needs to be done), and perseverance (to keep trying different approaches) are also essential.

These skills and concepts build on each other, helping students not only meet the specific standard but also laying the groundwork for more advanced mathematical learning.

This was helpful, but we decided that we needed to understand which aspects of this standard addressed conceptual knowledge and which focused on skills or methods. ChatGPT responded by organizing the first-grade math standard into two categories, as shown below in table 3.4.

Table 3.4: Categorization of First-Grade Math Standards into Conceptual Knowledge and Skills/Methods

Conceptual Knowledge	Skills/Methods
• Understanding of addition and subtraction • Number sense within 20 • Comparative reasoning and understanding concepts of comparison, like "more than," "less than," or "equal to"	• Solving word problems • Creating and using representations • Formulating equations • Dealing with unknowns in different positions • Mental math and strategies for addition and subtraction • Fluency with basic addition and subtraction facts • Problem-solving skills

With a clearer grasp of the standard itself, we prompted ChatGPT to articulate, in student-friendly language, a desired result for the standard. ChatGPT responded by suggesting the following student-friendly desired result.

By the end of our adventure together, you'll become super problem-solvers! You'll be able to listen to stories about friends sharing toys or cookies and figure out how many they have altogether or how many are left if someone takes some away. We'll learn to draw pictures, use our counting blocks, and even make up special number sentences with a mystery number to solve these fun puzzles. You'll become great at knowing your numbers up to 20 and be able to tell which group has more or fewer things. Get ready to play with numbers, solve mysteries, and become a number hero in our classroom!

This desired result was surely engaging for students, but we remembered that we needed to ensure that it was specific, measurable, relevant, attainable, and student-centered. Again, ChatGPT had us covered, offering the following breakdown:

Specific

- The outcome specifies what students will learn: solving problems based on stories, understanding addition and subtraction, using visual aids and manipulatives, identifying mystery numbers in equations, and comparing quantities.
- It mentions skills like drawing pictures, using counting blocks, and creating number sentences, which are specific strategies students will use.

Measurable

- The desired result implies measurability through actions students will take: listening to stories to solve math problems, drawing, and making up number sentences. These actions can be observed and assessed.
- However, it could be enhanced by explicitly stating how success will be measured, such as through specific examples of tasks or assessments.

Relevant

- The outcome is highly relevant, connecting math skills to real-life scenarios like sharing toys or cookies. This approach makes learning meaningful and applicable to students' experiences.
- It emphasizes number sense, problem-solving, and comparison skills, which are foundational for first-grade math and relevant to everyday situations.

Attainable

- The goals set are appropriate for first graders, focusing on foundational math skills within the 20-number range, which is consistent with educational standards for this age group.
- The outcome suggests a gradual learning process, starting with concrete manipulatives and moving toward more abstract number sentences, indicating a developmentally appropriate progression.

Student-Centered

- The language is student-centered, inviting learners into an "adventure" and framing their learning journey as becoming "super problem-solvers" and "number heroes." This language fosters engagement and positions students as active participants in their learning.

Several aspects of ChatGPT's guidance resonate strongly with our goals for outcome-oriented design. The emphasis on making the math problems relatable through real-life scenarios, like sharing toys or cookies, ensures relevance and would likely engage young learners. The student-friendly language (describing the learning journey as an "adventure" to become "super problem-solvers" and "number heroes") would likely foster excitement and position students as active agents in their learning, which aligns well with our student-centered approach.

The only missing element was to "explicitly state how success will be measured, such as through specific examples of tasks or assessments." Since the next step in backward design is to decide on an assessment strategy, we'll cross that bridge in the next chapter.

Table 3.5: Recap of Our Conversation with ChatGPT

Recap of Our Conversation with ChatGPT	
1.OA.A.1 Use addition and subtraction within 20 to solve word problems involving situations of adding to, taking from, putting together, taking apart, and comparing with unknowns in all positions, e.g., by using objects, drawings, and equations with a symbol for the unknown number to represent the problem.	
Unpack the Standard	Conceptual Knowledge • Understanding of addition and subtraction • Number sense within 20 • Comparative reasoning Methods/Skills • Solving word problems • Creating and using representations • Formulating equations • Dealing with unknowns in different positions • Mental math and strategies for addition and subtraction • Fluency with basic addition and subtraction facts • Problem-solving skills
Articulate the Desired Result	By the end of our adventure together, you'll become super problem-solvers! You'll be able to listen to stories about friends sharing toys or cookies and figure out how many they have altogether or how many are left if someone takes some away. We'll learn to draw pictures, use our counting blocks, and even make up special number sentences with a mystery number to solve these fun puzzles. You'll become great at knowing your numbers up to 20 and be able to tell which group has more or fewer things. Get ready to play with numbers, solve mysteries, and become a number hero in our classroom!

The Common Core Math Standards are dense, and a single standard may require that students understand and apply multiple concepts and skills. When we use AI to unpack standards, as shown in figure 3.1, we gain a clearer sense of what students will need to understand and be able to do. In a sense, ChatGPT breaks down the standard into its many parts, clarifying what must be included in a unit if we are going to help students demonstrate proficiency in that standard.

Like the first-grade math example, a standard can include many concepts and skills. Using a resource like the one pictured in figure 3.1 can guide the process of breaking down a standard or collection of standards so you can determine what students will need to be explicitly taught during the unit. This is critical pre-work, to be done before the teacher articulates a desired result for a unit of study, ensuring that the desired result is standards-aligned and creates a clear road map for teachers and students.

The work teachers do unpacking the standards to inform a strong desired result creates a strong foundation on which to build. It ensures that every lesson, learning activity, assignment, and assessment is purposefully directed toward a clear and meaningful outcome.

Figure 3.1: Design Template—Unpacking Standards and Crafting a Desired Result

Step 1: Unpacking the Standards

Content Standard[s]	
Concepts	
Skills	

What concepts or skills will students need to know or be able to do BEFORE the unit begins?	What concepts or skills will students need to know or be able to do DURING the unit to demonstrate proficiency in the standard?	How will students take the concepts and skills they learned and apply them at the END of the unit to demonstrate their learning?

Step 2: Crafting a Student-Friendly Desired Result

Desired Result	By the end of [name of the unit], students will [statement of how they will apply their learning].

One-Sentence Summary

Backward design emphasizes the importance of beginning with the end in mind by identifying desired results for units of study, and AI can aid educators in the process of unpacking standards and crafting specific, measurable, achievable, relevant, and student-centered desired results.

Reflect and Discuss

1. How do you currently design learning experiences? How much do you rely on your standards to drive your instruction?

2. How would unpacking the standards with the aid of AI help you to design learning experiences that more effectively target specific concepts and skills?

3. If you use an adopted curriculum, how might you apply the strategies in this chapter to identify the most important aspects of your curriculum and craft desired results you can share with your students?

4. How will crafting a desired result that can be shared with learners help to keep the work teachers and students do more focused and productive?

Time to Apply!

Let's put the strategies in this chapter to work as you begin to backward design your next unit!

- **Step 1:** Identify a standard(s) that you want to target in your next unit.
- **Step 2:** Use AI to unpack the standard, identifying its key concepts and skills. Find out what students need to know or be able to do at the start of the unit and what you'll need to explicitly teach them in the unit. Use the AI prompts in this

chapter to break down your standard(s) and develop your understanding of it.

Option: Use the template pictured in figure 3.1 to document what you are learning as you engage with AI.

- **Step 3:** Once you have unpacked your standard(s), use AI to generate a specific, measurable, achievable, relevant, and student-centered desired result to frame and focus your work during the unit. Use the prompts in this chapter to guide your work with AI to produce your desired result. Make sure to read through the suggested desired result and edit it to ensure it accurately conveys the learning goal of the unit.
- **Step 4:** Share your work with a colleague and ask for feedback about your desired result!

CHAPTER 4

Design an Assessment Strategy

Cross-Country College Tour Continued

Catlin   In the days leading up to our college tour on the East Coast, I told Cheyenne we needed a strategy for capturing our thoughts about each school. I knew the week was going to fly by in a blur of informational sessions with admissions officers and campus tours led by students. Since one outcome for this trip was to get a feel for each school and the surrounding area to determine whether Cheyenne could imagine herself spending four years there, I wanted to treat this experience like we were creating a documentary: I wanted Cheyenne to capture photos and identify aspects of each college that she liked or didn't like so we could use that information to guide us when she was knee-deep in the application process. Cheyenne opted to capture her experience using the journal app on her phone.

As we listened to admissions officers talk about each school's history, student-to-professor ratios, opportunities for undergrad research, tuition, financial aid, and what the university was looking for in a student, I took copious notes in Google Docs. By contrast,

Cheyenne listened with rapt attention and did not write a single thing down. Instead, she captured her thoughts at the end of each day in text and audio messages. The kid has a mind like a steel trap, so it didn't surprise me, but it reinforced the reality that everyone acquires and processes information in their own way!

It quickly became clear from our conversations that several things were important to Cheyenne. First, she loved campuses with beautiful, historic buildings with lots of stone or brick. Second, she was excited by schools that valued multidimensional students and encouraged them to pursue more than one area of concentration. Third, she was excited to do research as soon as possible and wanted to study abroad at some point in her college career. Last, she didn't enjoy the feeling of being on a college campus that was in the center of a big, bustling city.

To summarize, if we were making a rubric to assess each school, the criteria would include: 1) campus aesthetics, 2) multidimensional learning, 3) research opportunities and study abroad programs, and 4) campus location. By the end of our whirlwind week, Princeton was hands down the place Cheyenne felt she wanted to spend four years. It checked all her boxes. The campus was stunning, even on a gray, rainy day in April—check! She felt her love of science, literature, writing, and languages would all be nurtured there—check! They have a strong undergraduate focus and freshmen regularly get involved in research—check! And she loved the quaint little town of Princeton. It was just her speed. Check! She even raved about the campus bus system!

So, the great news was that in terms of desired results, the trip helped my high school junior figure out what she wanted in a college experience, specifically the criteria she would evaluate schools by. On the mommy-daughter front, the trip was also a resounding success. We talked for hours in the car and sang along to Taylor Swift, Olivia Rodrigo, and Ariana Grande's greatest hits as we drove from one school to the next. We enjoyed yummy meals and spent evenings curled up watching movies. As the trip came to an end, she gave me the biggest hug and said, "Thank you for doing this with me! It was so much fun! And now I have a dream school!" As a parent, it just doesn't get much better than that.

Just as Cheyenne and I developed a clear rubric to assess colleges based on the desired results of finding a university that was a good fit, teachers should move directly from identifying desired learning outcomes to designing an assessment strategy (complete with rubric). This will make them more likely to measure actual progress toward the desired results. By determining how success will be measured from the outset, teachers can ensure that every lesson, activity, and assessment aligns with the end goals, providing a cohesive and focused learning experience. This alignment not only helps in tracking student progress but also in making informed adjustments to teaching strategies to better meet the desired results—much like how our rubric guided Cheyenne's evaluation of each college.

Following our trip, AI was an invaluable tool in evaluating colleges that we couldn't visit in person. By inputting Cheyenne's criteria into ChatGPT, she received comprehensive data on each college, including student reviews, faculty profiles, and detailed information on programs and extracurricular opportunities. This AI-driven analysis allowed her to apply the same criteria she used during our trip to assess other schools, ensuring a thorough and consistent evaluation process.

Similarly, teachers can leverage AI to generate assessment strategies that accurately measure student progress toward desired results. AI can assist in creating standards-aligned rubrics, offering detailed feedback and examples, and suggesting diverse assessment methods that reflect students' varied learning preferences and needs. This not only simplifies the creation of assessment tools but also ensures they are robust, comprehensive, and tailored to the learning objectives.

Strong Pedagogical Practices

As we discussed in the previous chapter, the second step of backward design encourages educators and curriculum designers to move directly from articulating desired results to deciding on assessment evidence. In general, landing on an assessment strategy requires first considering three key questions:

- How will I measure how much progress my students have made toward the desired result?
- How will I ensure all my students can express and communicate their learning effectively?
- What types of assessments would be best for helping students to apply their learning in authentic ways?

UDL, like UbD, encourages us to develop assessment strategies that directly align with our desired results. Of course, even when a desired result is clearly stated, it's possible to provide multiple assessment options for students. These options are critical if the goal of assessing learning is to gain a clear and accurate understanding of what students know and can do. Instead of offering a single pathway for students to demonstrate their learning—such as a traditional multiple-choice test—we should strive to provide multiple pathways that remove potential barriers to students sharing their learning.

However, while it is important to offer multiple pathways for assessment as a matter of equity, supporting student agency and meaningful choice can create confusion and concern. For example, we often hear teachers question how they will grade assessments if students are creating different products or completing different tasks to demonstrate their learning. The implicit concern here is that grading will not (or could not) be fair if students do not all complete identical assessments. But with a clear desired result, the rubric we use to assess student learning will not change even if students create different assessment products.

Catlin faced a challenge around equitable assessments while coaching a high school history teacher who worked in an urban school with a diverse population of students. The teacher was preparing to wrap up a unit and wanted to assess how well students could answer its essential question, "What are the rights and responsibilities of citizens in a democratic society?" Students needed to support their answers with information gathered during the unit (content knowledge) by constructing a strong argument (skill set).

In the past, the teacher required her students to answer the question by writing an essay. But she was aware that this presented challenges for some of her students, especially her second-language learners. Some of her students wouldn't even attempt the essays and summarily earned zeros on assessments. When she spoke with them about why they had not completed the assessment, most told her that they "couldn't write an essay." When she probed them about the unit's content, several of those same students were able to answer the essential question verbally with some key details from the unit. So, the teacher knew her students could answer the question but realized that an essay was not going to work for them. She had also observed how artistic some of her students were on other assignments. She wished she could help them use their skills to effectively demonstrate their learning.

Armed with the knowledge that this one assessment pathway was not allowing all her students to share their learning accurately, the teacher decided to expand her students' options. Catlin and this teacher discussed the different artifacts students could produce to answer an essential question effectively and support their answers or claims with strong evidence from the unit. Together, they landed on three alternative assessments: an infographic, an essay, or a podcast, as shown in table 4.1.

Table 4.1: End-of-Unit Assessment Options

End-of-Unit Assessment

Select the product you want to create to answer the essential question for this unit. You need to support your answer with information and details from the unit. Your analysis and explanation must be organized and well developed.

Infographic	Written Response or Essay	Podcast or Recorded Speech
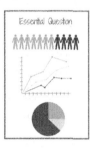		
Construct your visual response to this question with a clear claim and supporting evidence.	Compose a written response to answer the essential question for this unit.	Present your answer to the essential question in an oral presentation (e.g., recorded speech or podcast).
Select the medium for your infographic—paper or digital platform (e.g., Canva).	Include an introduction, body paragraph(s), and conclusion.	Your presentation should have a clear beginning, middle, and end.
Your answer to the question must include information from at least two sources and be clearly shown with images, drawings, connections (e.g., arrows), and keywords/phrases.	Support your statements with details and information from at least two sources, such as class lecture notes, primary/secondary source documents, videos/documentaries, podcast episodes, the textbook, etc.	Support your statements with details and information from at least two sources, such as class lecture notes, primary/secondary source documents, videos/documentaries, podcast episodes, the textbook, etc.
Your visual should reflect deep thinking, time and energy, and attention to detail.	Revise and edit your writing to ensure your statements are clear and organized.	Rehearse and refine your presentation to ensure it is practiced, professional, and clear.

Given the range of assessments on offer, the next question the history teacher asked was "If they submit different products, how will I grade that fairly?" It was clear to Catlin that the teacher was struggling to equate these assessments because she was getting bogged down in all the details of the individual products. Was the infographic aesthetically pleasing? Did it contain graphic displays of information? Did the essay reflect careful editing? Was the verbal explanation free from distracting filler words or background sounds? All of these were important attributes of the products, but they didn't necessarily reflect a given student's ability to answer the essential question.

Catlin asked the teacher to think about the desired result they had articulated for the unit: to answer the essential question, making a strong argument supported by details and information from the unit. From there, Catlin guided the teacher in identifying three criteria to include on her rubric that aligned with that desired result. They worked to create a four-point, mastery-based rubric that described what each criterion looked like at each level of mastery. The rubric they designed is pictured in table 4.2.

Table 4.2: Rubric for History Summative Assessment

Criteria	Beginning 1	Developing 2	Proficient 3	Mastery 4
Clarity of Claim	The product does not communicate a clear claim in response to the essential question.	The product attempts to present a claim in response to the essential question, but it would benefit from further detail and development.	The product presents a clear claim in response to the essential question, reflecting a firm understanding of the unit's content.	The product presents a clear and compelling claim in response to the essential question. The claim reflects a strong understanding of the unit's content.

Quality of Support and Evidence	Little to no concrete evidence was provided to support the points presented in the product. Factual information, quotes, and/ or details are needed.	Some evidence was provided to support the points presented in the product; however, the evidence needs to be stronger and more relevant to the central claim.	Strong evidence (e.g., factual information, quotes, and details) supported the central claim and the individual points presented in the product.	Compelling and strong evidence (e.g., factual information, quotes, and details) was provided throughout to support the central claim and the individual points presented in the product.
Clarity of Ideas and Organization	The product does not communicate a clear message. There is little evidence of organization.	The product attempts to communicate a response to the essential question; however, the organization of information needs revision to support the central claim.	The product communicates a clear response to the essential question, and the information is organized effectively to support the central claim.	The product clearly communicates a powerful response to the essential question and organizes information effectively to support the central claim.

Now, you may realize that the language of the initial rubric above is deficit-based. We have used rubrics like this throughout our careers, and all standardized tests use rubrics like this. This is how we were taught to create rubrics, and this is how ChatGPT will initially create them for us, which is one reason why we need to push back against AI when we use it as a tool for designing assessments. We never saw any issues with deficit-based rubrics until we had the opportunity to connect with the work of Shelley Moore,[1] a UDL expert and an advocate for the inclusion of students with the most significant intellectual support needs. Moore introduces the concept of the asset-based continuum as an alternative to the more deficit-based rubrics of current practice. Essentially, she poses a crucial question: Why would we want to highlight what students are *not* supposed to do instead of what they are capable of doing?

Shifting from a deficit-based rubric to an asset-based continuum can profoundly change how educational success is measured and encouraged. table 4.3 details how you might reframe your desired results into an asset-based continuum with three levels of complexity: essential, more complex, and even more complex. This continuum sets high expectations while acknowledging and building on each learner's strengths and achievements.

Table 4.3: Asset-Based Continuum

Criteria	Essential	More Complex	Even More Complex
Identification and Understanding of the Essential Question	Can identify the essential question of the unit	Can rephrase the essential question in their own words, showing a deeper understanding	Can expand on the essential question by connecting it to broader concepts or real-world issues, demonstrating higher-order thinking
Argument Construction	Makes a basic argument related to the essential question using simple details and information learned during the unit	Constructs a well-organized argument supported by detailed evidence and examples from the unit, showing critical thinking	Develops a nuanced and compelling argument, integrating complex details and information from the unit as well as outside sources, demonstrating sophisticated analysis

When teachers design a rubric or an asset-based continuum that aligns with their desired result and focuses the criteria on the specific standards driving the design of the unit of study, the type of artifacts students create to demonstrate their learning will not change how they are assessed. The goal is to measure student learning in alignment with firm, standards-aligned learning goals, and the pathway they select should not impact the rubric we use to assess their content knowledge and skill set.

AI Integration

The coaching session described above took place before AI became a significant force in education. Back then, it required considerable time to generate assessment products, descriptions, and a rubric. One of the great advantages of AI is that it can drastically reduce the time needed for these tasks. Even transforming rubrics into asset-based continuums can be accomplished in less than a minute!

While AI cannot replace the expertise and personalized guidance of a skilled coach, it offers a valuable alternative for educators who may not have access to professional coaching. AI can serve as a collaboration tool, providing support and resources to educators everywhere. Although concerns about AI replacing jobs are prevalent, the reality is that AI can complement the work of educators by making resources more accessible and efficient.

Let's revisit the desired results for the third-grade science and ninth-grade English language arts examples from chapter 3 and explore how AI can help you design your assessment strategy and provide flexible pathways. Table 4.4 will serve as a review.

Table 4.4: Examples of Desired Results

	Third-Grade Science	Ninth-Grade English Language Arts
Desired Result	• By the conclusion of our exploration of the rainforest ecosystem, students will be able to explain why some rainforest animals team up to stay safe and find food. They will use what they have learned to make a strong argument, showing how working together helps animals survive in the rainforest. • Students will research a specific animal group behavior and demonstrate their understanding by creating an artifact that makes an argument about how this behavior contributes to the survival and well-being of the group.	• By the end of our unit on empathy, students will be able to identify and analyze the central themes in short stories and the novel *To Kill a Mockingbird*. • Students will examine how a central theme emerges in the text and analyze its development through the narrative, focusing on specific details such as character actions, setting, and symbolism.

When we asked ChatGPT to suggest performance tasks that would effectively measure progress toward the above desired result for third-grade science, it provided a sizable nine options out of the gate:

- Group Presentation
- Digital Storytelling
- Infographic Design
- Role-Play Activity
- Research Paper or Essay
- Interactive Quiz or Game
- Field Study Report

- Scientific Poster Presentation

ChatGPT further provided robust descriptions of each assessment task and suggested the benefits of each one. Each task not only measures student progress toward understanding animal group behaviors and their survival benefits, but it also helps develop a range of skills like research, critical thinking, creativity, communication, and collaboration.

The problem is that nine options may create a barrier that prevents some students from being successful. One incredible paradox is that choice is necessary to minimize barriers to learning, but too many choices can create barriers due to choice paralysis. Research suggests that two to four choices is the sweet spot.[2] When using AI to generate performance tasks, there will be hits and misses. You know your students—their interests and preferences—so you can select a few options you think will best fit the learners in your class. Just be mindful, when you're striving to avoid choice paralysis, that you don't impose unnecessary limits.

The most important thing to remember is that if we don't provide flexible options, some students may face barriers that prevent them from meeting a standard. When we consider requiring every student to complete a research paper, we must acknowledge potential obstacles to success, such as writer's block and challenges with grammar, punctuation, or fluency. However, by recognizing that the primary goal is not solely to assess writing skills but to understand what students understand about a subject, we can create more inclusive pathways.

To effectively design these pathways, educators can leverage the GRASPS (goal, role, audience, situation, performance, standard) design tool developed by Grant Wiggins and Jay McTighe as part of their work on UbD. This tool helps craft authentic and meaningful performance tasks, encouraging students to apply their learning in real-world scenarios.

As you look through the suggestions presented by ChatGPT, you will note a presentation format that encourages peer collaboration, a scientific poster for those who lean toward visual and artistic expression, and a field study report that offers a hands-on approach to learning. Once you select three to four options, you are ready to ask ChatGPT to apply the GRASPS design tool.

Deciding to push ChatGPT further, we asked it to apply GRASPS principles specifically to the scientific poster presentation option. AI supplied the following breakdown for us:

Scientific Poster Presentation

- Goal: Create an informative and visually appealing scientific poster about a specific animal group behavior.
- Role: You are a biologist who has conducted extensive research on a particular animal group behavior.
- Audience: Your audience is fellow scientists and students at a scientific conference.
- Situation: You need to convey your findings and explain how this behavior contributes to the survival of the species.
- Performance: Your poster should include an introduction to the behavior, its significance, visual aids (like diagrams or photographs), and a conclusion highlighting the survival benefits.
- Standards: The poster should be scientifically accurate, well-organized, visually engaging, and include references to your research sources.

ChatGPT replicated this same breakdown for each of the other performance tasks. Its suggestions were strong across the board but not necessarily appropriate for students in the third grade. So, we asked it to recalibrate accordingly.

From ChatGPT's revised suggestions, we constructed the assessment choice board shown in table 4.5. You'll notice that we made further adjustments to meet the needs of a group of third-grade students. Remember, one goal of UDL is to give students meaningful choices as they approach assessment and to remove barriers that might interfere with their ability to communicate and express what they learned. With that in mind, we made sure to provide students with the agency to decide which animal group and behavior they wanted to focus on and included options for students to work alone or with a partner on certain assessments. We know that some students may enjoy more tactile tasks, while others enjoy using technology and online tools, so we also gave students choice and voice around the materials to use for their products.

Table 4.5: Third-Grade Science Assessment Choice Board

Third-Grade Science: Performance Task Choice Board
Directions: Select an animal group you are interested in focusing on for this assessment. You can choose bees, fish, lions, wolves, or any other animal group you are interested in. Decide how you want to demonstrate what you've learned about your animal group and how their behavior helps them survive.

Scientific Poster	**Short Story**
Imagine you are a young scientist who knows a lot about a specific animal group and its behavior. Design an informative poster about the animal group's behavior. What do these animals do? Why do they do it? How does this behavior help them to survive? Include images and/or drawings to help your classmates understand your animal group and their behavior.	Imagine you are a writer using stories to teach children about animal groups and how they work together to survive. Write a story that focuses on the animal group's behavior. What do these animals do? Why do they do it? How does this behavior help them to survive? Include interesting details and characters that show what you have learned and will engage your classmates.
Options: • Work on your own or with a partner. • Use poster paper and markers or an online design tool like Canva.	Options: • Write on your own or with a partner. • Type or write your story by hand or record an audio track reading your story.

Field Study Report	**Group Presentation**
Imagine you are a detective investigating how animals act. You'll need to observe an animal group (in person or in videos). Create a report that mixes images, drawings, and writing to share what you learned about your animal group's behavior. What do these animals do? Why do they do it? How does this behavior help them to survive? Include specific details from your observations in your report. Options: • Work on your own or with a partner. • Create your report on paper or on a Google Slides deck.	Imagine you're the teacher for a day, teaching the class about a specific animal group's behavior. Create an engaging presentation for the class about how animals work together to help each other survive. What do these animals do? Why do they do it? How does this behavior help them to survive? Include facts in your presentation and have the class do something with the information you share (e.g., turn-and-talk questions or activity). Options: • Work with a partner or a small group of up to four classmates. • Decide how you want to share information—live or as a recorded video.

AI-Enhanced Rubric Design

Designing rubrics with descriptions of what learning looks like at every level of mastery takes time, or it did before AI! Now, teachers have access to a powerful rubric generator that whips up the language so you can focus on editing and refining it for your students. An overview of the process we use to design rubrics or asset-based continuums appears in table 4.6.

Once teachers have created an assessment strategy that will allow them to measure student progress toward the desired results, we suggest creating the rubric or the asset-based continuum you will use to assess students. In her book *Balance with Blended Learning*, Catlin discusses the value of designing descriptive rubrics with clear explanations of what performance looks like at each level of mastery.[3] Not only do these descriptions help students understand what is expected of them, but they make the rubric a powerful self-assessment tool. We encourage teachers to create and share rubrics with students at the start of a unit or learning cycle so they can guide learners' work, encourage self-assessment, and support a reflective and metacognitive practice.

Table 4.6: AI-Enhanced Rubric Design Process

AI-Enhanced Rubric or Asset-Based Continuum Design Process	
Step 1	Revisit the desired results and target standards to get clear on what students will need to know or be able to do at the end of the unit. Tell AI what the desired result is for a unit of study and include the target standards driving the design of your unit. Then, ask what standards-aligned criteria it would suggest you include in a rubric designed to assess student progress toward this desired result.
Step 2	Select the three to five criteria you want to include on your standards-aligned rubric and edit the AI-generated language for your students to ensure they understand the criteria.
Step 3	**For a rubric**, ask AI to describe what learning/performance looks like at each level of mastery (beginning, developing, proficiency, mastery) and remind it to write the descriptions in student-friendly language.
	For an asset-based continuum, ask AI to describe what learning/ performance looks like at three levels of complexity: essential, more complex, and even more complex, framing student performance in positive language focused on what they are able to do (not what they failed to do).
Step 4	Edit the language as needed to ensure clarity and usability.

Let's take the science assessment above and design a rubric that a third-grade teacher could use to assess any of those four products—scientific poster, presentation, field study report, or short story. First, we need to revisit our desired result. Next, we need to identify the specific criteria we want to assess that are focused on the key conceptual knowledge and processes identified in the Next Generation

Science Standard 3-LS2-1. So, let's return to ChatGPT to get guidance on the criteria we might want to include in our rubric, asking it to take both the standard and our assessment options into account. ChatGPT identifies the following criteria, provides a description of what each criterion looks like at each level of mastery, and suggests point allocations for each criterion:

- Understanding the Content
- Application of Knowledge
- Communication
- Creativity and Innovation

Drawing on our own experience and expertise—remember, AI is a collaborator, not a decision-maker—we decided to deviate from ChatGPT's suggestions slightly. Some suggestions may not feel specific enough, or they may be too subjective. So, we chose to focus on the following criteria:

- Understanding of Animal Group's Behaviors
- Evidence
- Clarity of Ideas and Organization

Since this assessment is focused on an animal group's behaviors, we made the language for that criterion more specific. Instead of focusing on applying knowledge to produce an artifact, we wanted to focus on how well students supported their arguments and ideas with information and evidence gathered during the unit. We also chose to replace "Communication" with "Clarity of Ideas and Organization" since no matter what product they created, students would need to organize the information and present their ideas to an audience. Finally, we chose not to use "Creativity and Innovation," which felt too subjective.

When coaching teachers, we usually suggest they limit the criteria they include on a rubric. Too many items can create a tremendous amount of work for you, and it may also be hard for students to process that many individual assessment scores. Thus, we encourage you to limit your criteria to three to five for everyone's sake!

Building on the criteria we landed on, table 4.7 is an example of a traditional rubric we can use to assess the performance tasks students complete to demonstrate their learning.

Table 4.7: NGSS 3-LS2-1 NGSS Science Rubric

Criteria	Beginning 1	Developing 2	Proficient 3	Mastery 4
Understanding of animal group's behaviors	The explanation of animal group behavior is unclear or largely incorrect. Shows a limited understanding.	Provides a basic explanation of animal group behavior, but there are some mistakes and/ or missing details. Shows an incomplete understanding.	Provides a mostly accurate explanation of animal group behavior with minor mistakes. The explanation shows a good understanding.	Provides a clear and accurate explanation of animal group behavior and how it helps members survive. The explanation is detailed and shows a deep understanding.

Evidence	Provides little to no evidence to support the argument about animal behavior and how it helps them survive. Few, if any, facts or specific examples.	Provides limited evidence to support the argument about animal behavior and how it helps them survive. Includes a few facts and examples.	Provides some evidence to support their argument about animal behavior and how it helps them survive. Includes good facts and examples to explain why animals behave this way.	Provides multiple, well-chosen pieces of evidence (e.g., examples, facts, or data) to support the argument about animal behavior and how it helps them survive. Includes lots of good facts and specific examples to explain why animals behave this way.
Clarity of ideas and organization	Ideas are unclear and unorganized, which makes it challenging to understand the information presented.	Ideas are somewhat clear but lack organization and/or contain several vocabulary errors or misused animal terms.	Ideas are presented clearly with small errors in terms of clarity, organization, or vocabulary.	Ideas are presented clearly with logical organization and effectively using vocabulary and animal terms.

As we discussed above, however, this version of our rubric takes a mostly deficit-based approach. Teachers interested in transitioning from traditional deficit-based rubrics to an asset-based continuum can simply submit their traditional rubrics to ChatGPT as an image file with the following prompt:

Catlin and Katie: Create an asset-based continuum as an alternative to this traditional rubric. I'd like the asset-based continuum to describe what learning/performance looks like at three levels of complexity: essential, more complex, and even more complex, using language a third-grade student can understand and framing student performance in positive language. Focus on what they are able to do (not what they failed to do). The three criteria we are including in the asset-based continuum are: [insert criteria].

When we provided guidance with our rubric, AI did the heavy lifting for us and suggested the following asset-based continuum, pictured in table 4.8.

Table 4.8: Asset-Based Continuum for Assessing NGSS 3-LS2-1

Asset-Based Continuum for understanding Animal Group Behaviors			
Criteria	Complex	More Complex	Even More Complex
Understanding of Animal Group Behaviors	The student identifies key behaviors of animal groups and explains their basic significance to survival, demonstrating foundational understanding.	The student describes animal group behaviors with greater detail and recognizes the various functions of these behaviors in supporting the group's survival, showing a clear understanding.	The student describes complex interactions within animal group behaviors and explains the specific ways these behaviors contribute to the survival and thriving of the group, reflecting a strong understanding.

Evidence	The student provides clear examples or information to show the relationship between animal behaviors and survival.	The student provides a range of evidence, including specific examples, information, and data to support their argument about animal behaviors and survival.	The student provides strong evidence, including specific examples, detailed information, and data to strengthen and support their argument about animal behaviors and survival.
Clarity of Ideas and Organization	The student expresses ideas in a way that communicates their understanding, using vocabulary related to animal behaviors.	The student organizes and presents ideas in a clear way, demonstrating a definite progression of thought, and uses vocabulary that strengthens the clarity and the explanation of animal behaviors.	The student clearly organizes their ideas, communicating complex concepts with specific vocabulary, showing a strong understanding of the relationships within animal group behaviors.

Regardless of the types of tools used to assess students, it is critical that they be grounded in the standards and desired results so that we can provide students with flexible pathways to express and communicate their learning effectively.

One-Sentence Summary

By leveraging AI to generate assessment strategies, educators can create flexible pathways that offer diverse learners authentic, meaningful assessments aligned with learning standards and desired results.

Reflect and Discuss

1. Reflect on your current assessment practices. How do you ensure that your assessments align with the desired results of your instruction? What challenges have you faced in creating assessments that accurately measure student learning?

2. Considering the diverse needs of your students, how could offering multiple assessment options (e.g., infographics, podcasts) impact their ability to demonstrate their understanding? How might this approach change your assessment strategies?

3. How do you view the role of AI in creating assessments and rubrics? Share an instance where integrating technology into assessment design could have or did enhance the learning experience for you and your students.

4. This chapter presents a shift from deficit-based to asset-based assessment rubrics. How might this shift influence your approach to assessment? Discuss the potential impacts on student motivation and self-assessment skills.

Time to Apply!

Let's put the strategies in this chapter to work as you design an assessment strategy and rubric or asset-based continuum to assess student progress toward the desired result you articulated at the end of chapter 3!

- **Step 1:** Revisit your desired result and think about how you can measure student progress toward that desired result.
- **Step 2:** Use AI to help you generate flexible pathways for this assessment to ensure all students can demonstrate mastery. How might students demonstrate that they understand key concepts or can apply specific skills? Use the AI prompts in this chapter to generate a "would you rather" option with

two meaningful choices or a four-option choice board for students to select from to demonstrate their learning.

- **Step 3:** Once your "would you rather" or choice board is complete, use the rubric or asset-based continuum template included in the resources for this book to create your standards-aligned rubric or continuum to measure student progress toward the desired results.
- **Step 4:** Share your work with a colleague and ask for feedback about your assessment strategy and rubric or continuum!

PART II

Designing for Equity

Design Path

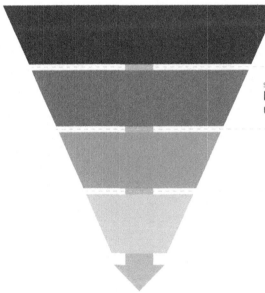

STEP 1
Identify Desired Results
Align Desired Results and Assessment Strategy

STEP 2
Design Equitable Learning Experiences
Universally Designed Blended Learning

CHAPTER 5

Designing Equitable Learning Experiences

Runaway Train

Katie My sister Lindie and I both married skiers. Growing up, we never tried skiing or had any interest in doing so, and after a while, enough time had passed that we considered ourselves non-skiers. Our husbands taught our kids to ski when they were in preschool while we only recently learned to ski ourselves.

I will never forget the first time we decided to meet in the evening to ski. We took a half day at work, drove to the mountain, and got on the ski lift. When we got to the top, I rolled off the lift, tangled myself in my skis, and realized it probably wasn't a great move to come to the top of the mountain without any idea of how to get down. Lindie, always a better athlete than me, immediately took off like a bat out of hell, swerving around a group of small children in ski school. By the time I got up on my skis, went into an aggressive pizza stance to slow myself down, and scraped by the small children, my sissy was nowhere in sight. In my internal dialogue, I went back to high school jealousy that she was so magically good at everything while also thinking I was incredibly impressed that she had the speed of Mikaela Shiffrin as she zoomed down the mountain.

It took me a couple of minutes to make it that two hundred yards, sacrificing myself to a fall every ten seconds because I felt like I was going too fast. That is when I heard Lindie's voice coming from the woods. Apparently, soon after takeoff, she spun out of control, lost her skis and poles (called a *yard sale* in ski speak), and rolled down into the trees. Luckily, she had on her helmet and was perfectly OK, but as I saw her clutching branches to climb back up onto the ski trail, I laughed so hard that I cried.

So, why am I telling this story? Ski resorts are often brilliantly universally designed, and there are options and choices for everyone. At any time during our trips to the mountains, we could have signed up for a lesson, chosen the bunny slope, enrolled in the adult learn-to-ski program, or even taken an alternative path like snowshoeing or having a beer in the lodge. But here's the thing. We didn't.

With its emphasis on access and equity, UDL underscores the importance of understanding the potential barriers people may face and ensuring they have the options and choices they need to reach desired results (i.e., enjoy time at the ski resort). But goodness, not everyone makes responsible decisions all the time. This is why UDL practitioners must be responsive and self-aware. In the chapters that follow, we'll explore how to create a learning space that is accessible to all. Along the way, we'll learn best practices for building relationships, providing instruction and feedback, and supporting learner agency.

Strong Pedagogical Practices

UDL: More than Choice and Voice

Universal Design is grounded in architecture. When a building is universally designed, every member of the public has a pathway to enter the building and purposefully engage with all spaces within that building. The first step in the design process is to consider the goals of the building and the purpose of the space. Why would somebody come in and utilize that space? These are the firm goals—desired results—that we spoke about in the previous chapters. But once you know the intended use of a space, you must design it so that everyone has the same opportunities to reach those goals.

For example, imagine a group of architects designing a bank. They recognize that it will be important for every member of the public to be able to access the ATM, the office spaces where they fill out loan applications, and the cashier's desk. Now, imagine that the cashiers are working at countertop height, and the hallway leading to the personal offices is not wide enough for a wheelchair. We can even think of the outside of the bank and imagine how a curb, a cobblestone walkway, or a set of stairs might similarly create barriers for some people. This bank becomes inaccessible to users who have mobility needs, such as people who are in wheelchairs, those who may be pushing a baby stroller, or those who may struggle in other ways. Now, this bank may provide numerous options to customers, such as different types of accounts and loans, and they may be open to feedback. In this instance, while the bank fosters choice and voice, it is simply not accessible to everyone, so it is not universally designed.

Often, teachers consider UDL a framework that fosters voice and choice. However, it's critical to understand that flexibility and options are also meant to ensure that every single learner can access a lesson and work toward rigorous grade-level goals; voice and choice simply aren't enough to assure equity. Too often, teachers say that they are using UDL already, but the quality of Universal Design should not be measured in the intentions of the designer but rather in the impact that design has on all the learners.

Too often, teachers say that they are using UDL already, but the quality of Universal Design cannot be measured in the intentions of the designer but rather in the impact that design has on all the learners.

There's a great story about Hunters Point Library in Queens, New York. A group of brilliant architects spent a decade and nearly $42 million to create a space that the public could enjoy. The intention, of course, was that people, regardless of their needs, would be able to access the library with all its terraces and that all children would be able to enjoy the children's section. Although the intention was to universally design the building, however, there were three significant design flaws that became apparent once the library opened: many people could not access the terraces, the children's section had bleachers that were so steep they were deemed dangerous, and there was only a single elevator to serve all five floors.[1]

This anecdote pairs so well with misconceptions about UDL, its implementation in the classroom, and its impact on students. We have no doubt that educators are well intentioned, like the architects of Hunters Point Library. That said, the flexibility and accommodations necessary for some people to learn at high levels are often unavailable or available only to a certain few. This unnecessary limitation is not representative of UDL's ideals.

We know that we serve learners who have varying needs. We can expect that we will serve students who need acceleration and support, possibly in multiple domains—academic, behavioral, social/emotional, linguistic, and cultural. We know this is a lot to consider, but we also know that it is predictable. Therefore, we need to design for it.

Universal Design in teaching demands that we design educational experiences not only for the students we *currently* serve but also for the variability of *any students* we may serve. We often talk to educators who are incredibly talented and create a space where the students they work with make significant progress. However, there are many students who simply do not have access to these educators' classrooms because they are placed in lower levels or substantially separate settings—classrooms or schools entirely dedicated to students with special education support needs, as opposed to inclusive settings where students with and without disabilities learn together. If a student who does not yet know English, a student who has significant intellectual support needs, or a student who is blind joined your class, can you confidently say that your lesson is adaptable enough to meet their needs? If it is not, it is not universally designed.

So, you may be wondering how the process of Universal Design differs if you have district-required materials. First, we hope that if you have adopted high-quality instructional materials (HQIM), some UDL elements are already in place, as curriculum designers are often proactive in determining potential barriers and providing access to options to eliminate them. However, even if UDL is not a component of required materials, you still have choices for better meeting the needs of all learners.

For example, in HQIM, students are often asked to access text, videos, or audio. To read texts, students could work alone or with a partner, print out hard copies or find digital access. When accessing materials digitally, students could choose to read aloud. When prompted to respond to a text, students could do so in writing, but they may need access to a graphic organizer, a peer review session, or a way to view and deconstruct an example. UDL-infused class discussions may require educators to provide an option to activate background knowledge, review sentence stems, or choose how to participate in a discussion—for example, a fishbowl or a small-group discussion with roles like moderator, notetaker, timekeeper, etc.

Teachers can employ strong pedagogical practices to implement UDL while using required HQIM with integrity. This approach ensures that all students, regardless of their learning preferences or needs, have equitable access to the curriculum, thereby supporting a more inclusive learning environment.

Blended Learning: It's More than Technology

While UDL has a specific origin in architecture, the advent of blended learning cannot be attributed to a single event or innovation but rather the gradual integration of technology into education. In fact, the roots of blended learning can be traced back to distance education, which has been around since the nineteenth century. Early forms of distance education utilized correspondence courses, and as technology evolved, so did the methods of delivery. Early distance education relied on packets of printed materials, and then it evolved to rely on radio and television channels, then cassette and video tapes, and eventually the internet.

The popularity of distance education, particularly correspondence courses, reflected the diverse needs and circumstances of learners. For some, geographic location was a hurdle. Individuals living in remote or rural areas may not have had access to educational institutions because of the sheer distance, time required to travel, cost, and even lack of transportation infrastructure. For many, the appeal of distance education lay in its flexibility and convenience, catering to those with demanding work schedules, family responsibilities, and health concerns or physical disabilities. Distance education allowed people to study and further their education on their own schedule and at a pace that worked for them. Distance education also provided people access to specialized programs or courses that may not have been offered locally, allowing learners to pursue niche interests or career-specific training courses.

Blended learning's origin in distance education is important because it highlights its fundamental value even today. The appeal of these courses was accessibility, flexibility, and personalization—all features of online learning. But relying solely on the addition of technology to learning still poses challenges. Technology is great for *some* applications that previously required human time, energy, and expertise. For example, we can record instruction and curate online reading materials, making them available for people to watch and read digitally. We can automate assessments to quickly measure student understanding and chart progress. Yet learning is fundamentally social. Students may need individual instruction, support, and feedback to understand complex concepts or apply specific skills. They benefit from engaging in discussions with peers, learning from different perspectives, and enjoying a space to ask questions. The role of students as active agents interacting with other members of a learning community is critical to their engagement and motivation.

Massive open online courses (MOOCs) underscore the limitations of technological innovation for educational transformation. MOOCs originated in the late 2000s as an evolution of distance education, leveraging the internet to provide wide-scale access to educational opportunities. The goal for MOOCs was to democratize education by providing access to courses from prestigious universities and institutions to anyone with a computer and an internet connection. Like early distance courses, MOOCs are accessible, flexible, and offer learners the opportunity to personalize their learning experience by selecting specific courses in areas of interest.

MOOCs have been incredibly successful at attracting students, as evidenced by the millions of learners who have signed up for online courses. However, MOOCs have faced challenges retaining students after the first few weeks of initial enthusiasm wanes. In fact, retention rates for MOOCs fall in the range of 3 percent and 15 percent, with 90 percent of students failing to complete the courses they are enrolled in.[2] So, lots of students sign up for MOOCs, but very few ever finish their coursework.

Given the potential of MOOCs to make education more accessible, flexible, and personalized, researchers have tried to understand the factors causing these low levels of course completion. Myriad personal or logistic reasons may be to blame, but we believe that design is at the heart of the issue. In a study exploring more learner-centered approaches to MOOCs, researchers noted that the "pedagogical design limitations in MOOCs are known to result in passive role of the learner, lack of learner connect and engagement, limited interactivity with course content and peers, all of which result in low completion rates."[3] Ultimately, many MOOCs position learners as passive consumers who take in information with limited, if any, opportunities to interact with an instructor. MOOCs also lack a learning community to help students process their learning, engage in conversation, seek clarification, and receive feedback on their work in progress.

Technology itself isn't enough, but blended learning is so much more than just technology. That's why blended learning provides an exciting reimagining of the traditional, one-size-fits-all approach to instruction that is still used in classrooms all over the globe. Blended learning is the combination of active, engaged learning online and active, engaged learning offline to give students more control over the time, place, pace, and path of their learning. The goal of blended learning is to position the student as an active agent in education by shifting from a teacher-centered to a student-centered approach to teaching and learning.

Many educators wrongly believe that blended learning *requires* online learning outside of the physical classroom. Blended learning absolutely can involve a hybrid schedule, but it doesn't have to. What matters is that educators use technology intentionally. So, when we talk about blended learning, we are focused on how we can achieve specific goals with technology-enhanced instructional models:

1. **Make learning accessible.** Give students autonomy and agency by providing flexible pathways through a lesson or learning experience.
2. **Differentiate and personalize learning.** Ensure students receive the necessary teacher time and energy to ensure an equitable learning experience.
3. **Connect the members of a learning community.** Support students as they make progress toward learning objectives and desired results.

Blended learning models, pictured in figure 5.1, should serve as instructional structures that provide educators with multiple options for designing lessons that accomplish these goals.

Figure 5.1: Taxonomy of Blended Learning Models

Teacher is the driver of design, instruction, and facilitation

Online learning is the driver, with instruction delivered digitally

The Rotation Models	Flex Model	A la Carte Model	Enriched Virtual Model

 Station Rotation Model

 Flipped Classroom Model

Whole-Group Rotation Model

 Playlist/Individual Rotation Model

As the diagram suggests, there are several formats for blended learning models. To select the best one for a particular lesson or lesson sequence, teachers must consider a variety of factors. Table 5.2 focuses on the four rotation models which work well in a traditional classroom. Here, we've suggested the questions you should ask of each model, and we've highlighted the benefits of each for both teachers and students. Ultimately, taking time to consider these questions will help educators design the most effective learning experiences that provide the necessary student control over time, place, pace, and path of their learning.

Table 5.1: Selecting the Best Blended Learning Model[4]

Blended Learning Rotation Models	Points to Consider	The Benefits
The Flipped Classroom Model	• Does the teacher plan to present the information the same way for everyone? • Is the information dense or complex? Would students benefit from pausing or rewinding? • Is this information that students typically need repeat exposure to?	• Students control the pace of their progress, pausing, rewinding, rewatching, or adjusting the speed of the video. • Students can access features that improve their ability to acquire information (e.g., closed captioning or transcript).

| The Station Rotation Model | • Are students in different places in terms of their prior knowledge or skill set?
• Does pre-assessment, diagnostic, or formative assessment data indicate students have different instructional needs?
• Will the instruction or modeling sessions benefit from differentiation in small groups?
• Are students working on a product that would benefit from focused, actionable teacher feedback?
• Are there learning activities that would benefit from collaborative or peer-to-peer learning?
• Would specific learning tasks work better as individual or small-group tasks? | • Teachers have dedicated time to work with small groups of learners to differentiate instruction and modeling sessions, which is ideal if students have different levels of prior knowledge, language proficiencies, or skill and abilities.
• Teachers can use their small-group time to provide focused, actionable feedback as students work.
• Students have a higher degree of control over their progress when working at the other stations.
• Students engage with a mix of online and offline, individual and collaborative tasks, integrating multiple modes of learning into a lesson. |

| The Whole-Group Rotation Model | • Are there activities that would benefit from the class engaging simultaneously because they generate significant noise or movement in the classroom?

• Is there instruction or a modeling session the teacher wants to present the same way for all students in class so the teacher can gauge understanding or be available for questions?

• Does the teacher want all students to spend time working online with an adaptive software or personalized learning program?

• Are there students who need additional support or reteaching on a topic or skill? | • Teachers can engage the whole class in offline learning activities that may generate noise or require physical movement around the room (e.g., four-corner conversations).

• If the teacher is unable to make a video or rely on other forms of media to transfer information to the whole class, they can provide that instruction or model to the class in real time.

• As students self-pace through personalized pathways with an online program, the teacher can use that time to pull individual or small groups for additional instruction, support, or reteaching. |

| The Playlist Model | • Are students working on a multi-step task or product that requires variable time, with some students progressing much more quickly or slowly?
• Would students benefit from personalized instruction, support, and feedback as they work? | • Students have control over their learning pace as they work through tasks that take variable amounts of time to complete.
• The model allows teachers to delegate the delivery of basic information to videos and other multimedia resources, freeing them to concentrate on personalized and differentiated instruction, working directly with individual students or small groups who need additional instruction, support, or scaffolding.
• Students hone their self-directed learning skills as they own more of the responsibility for their learning. |

AI Integration

Educators often struggle to imagine how to eliminate the many barriers to learning, but the UDL Guidelines provide a tool that highlights predictable barriers and offers strategies to address them. Designing a UDL lesson presents challenges, particularly when integrating the diverse needs of students into a cohesive plan. Operationalizing these lessons through blended learning adds another layer of complexity, requiring educators to seamlessly combine online and face-to-face instructional methods. However, by using AI in conjunction with the UDL Guidelines, educators can efficiently design lessons that cater to diverse learner needs. AI can offer personalized resources and suggestions, helping to implement the strategies recommended by the UDL Guidelines. The latest version, UDL Guidelines 3.0, released in July 2024, addresses biases and exclusion in education, aiming to design learning environments that respect and value every learner.[5]

The prompts below will help you to use ChatGPT effectively as you design lessons with UDL and blended learning principles in mind. In particular, we've offered suggestions for focusing on multiple means of engagement, representation, and action and expression while ensuring that all flexibility is construct-relevant. Construct relevance means all assessment pathways and instructional methods align directly with the learning standards and desired outcomes. That way, variations in approach do not compromise the essential skills and knowledge being assessed. These prompts are crafted to create a learning environment that accommodates the diverse needs of learners.

> ### *Keyword Alert!*
> **Multiple means of engagement:** Learners' interests and sources of motivation can vary depending on the context. Some learners are highly engaged by spontaneity and novelty, while others find these aspects disengaging or even triggering, preferring a strict routine. Some learners enjoy working alone, while others prefer collaborating with peers. These preferences can vary from week to week or even day to day. There is no single means of engagement that will be optimal for all learners in every context; therefore, providing multiple options for engagement is essential.

Multiple Means of Engagement

- Prompt for welcoming interests and identities: "How can I design assessments that align with [specific standard or desired result] and welcome students' interests and identities to increase motivation and engagement?"

- Prompt for designing options that sustain effort and persistence: "What strategies or technologies can help students sustain effort and persistence while working toward [specific standard]. What design options encourage continued engagement and resilience?"

- Prompt for designing options for emotional capacity: "How can I create a lesson that supports students' emotional capacity as they engage with [specific standard], ensuring they have the tools to manage emotions and stress effectively?"

Let's try these out with our pal, ChatGPT. Imagine you are working toward a history standard:

Explain the development of colonial governments and describe how these developments (e.g., legislative bodies, town meetings, and charters on individual freedoms and rights) contributed to the Revolution.

Provided with this standard, ChatGPT suggested four assessment options:

- Personalized Project Choices: Allow students to choose from various project formats, such as creating a short film, a graphic novel, or a digital presentation, that explore how the development of colonial governments contributed to the Revolution. Encourage them to incorporate elements that reflect their cultural backgrounds or personal interests, such as relating historical events to their family history or community stories.

- Cultural Connections Essay: Assign students to write an essay connecting colonial governance developments with their cultural or personal identities. For instance, students could explore parallels between colonial charters and freedoms with governance structures in their cultural heritage, allowing them to engage with the material from a personal perspective.

- Identity-Based Role-Playing: Organize a role-playing activity where students assume roles of diverse historical figures or marginalized groups affected by colonial governance changes. Encourage students to draw connections between these historical experiences and contemporary issues they are passionate about.

- Interactive Exhibit Design: Have students design an interactive exhibit (physical or virtual) that showcases the evolution of colonial governments and their impact on the Revolution. Allow students to incorporate artifacts, narratives, and media that resonate with their personal interests or cultural identities, making the history more relatable and engaging.

Given the level of work needed to complete any of these assessments, we realized that our students may require additional support to sustain effort and persistence. So, we asked ChatGPT for advice on that front. It offered the following:

- Structured Check-ins and Reflections: Schedule regular check-ins with students to discuss their progress, challenges, and reflections. This keeps them accountable and provides opportunities for personalized feedback and encouragement.

- Goal Setting and Self-Assessment: Encourage students to set specific, measurable goals for their projects and regularly assess their progress toward these goals. This fosters a sense of ownership and helps maintain motivation.

- Peer Collaboration and Feedback: Facilitate peer review sessions where students can share their work and receive constructive feedback. This not only enhances the quality of their work but also builds a supportive classroom community.

ChatGPT, you knock our socks off! All three of those strategies align with the principles of UDL. They're strong pedagogical practices, but teachers may struggle to implement them in the classroom. This is where blended learning comes in! By incorporating ChatGPT's suggested support activities as part of a rotation model, you can create the time and space for structured check-in time with small groups of learners while other students perform self-assessments or collaborate with their peers.

For example, table 5.2 shows a station rotation lesson with four separate stations designed to allow students to make progress on their assessments with support. Because students will have made progress on their assessments prior to this station rotation, they can begin at any station.

Table 5.2: Station Rotation Lesson: Supporting Authentic Assessments

Station Rotation Lesson: Supporting Authentic Assessments	
Station 1: Teacher-Led Check-in & Feedback	**Station 2: Self-Assessment & Reflection**
As the group works on their assessment, the teacher meets individually with students to check on their progress and provide focused, actionable, process-based feedback on their work.	Students engage in a self-assessment activity, using the rubric provided by the teacher to assess their current performance in relation to each criterion. After assessing their work, they complete a reflection identifying areas of strength and areas in need of improvement or development.
Station 3: Peer Feedback & Collaboration	**Station 4: Work Time!**
Students exchange work with a peer and provide kind, specific, and substantive feedback using a peer feedback choice board. They can write their feedback to each other or provide it verbally. Then, students work to incorporate the feedback they've been given.	Students continue to work on their assessments, and they can access peer support if needed.

Multiple Means of Representation

Just as we used AI prompts to find supports that increase student engagement, we can also use them to find suggestions for incorporating multiple means of representation.

Keyword Alert!

Multiple means of representation: Learners process information in different ways. For example, people with sensory disabilities like blindness or deafness, learning challenges like dyslexia, and those from diverse cultural or linguistic backgrounds engage with content differently. It's essential to acknowledge and value these differences by ensuring learners have multiple ways to access and engage with content, ultimately enhancing their ability to build and apply knowledge.

For this exercise, we'll share the same standard as the previous section and then ask the following:

- Prompt for designing options for perception: "What are various ways to present [specific standard] that ensure it is accessible to students with different sensory needs?"
- Prompt for designing options for language and symbols: "How can I explain [specific standard] using multiple representations like symbols, language, and visual aids to cater to diverse linguistic backgrounds?"
- Prompt for designing options for building knowledge: "How can I incorporate multiple ways of building individual and collective knowledge when working toward [specific standard]?"

To present the standard to students with different sensory needs, consider the following approaches:

Audiovisual materials: Incorporate videos and podcasts that detail the era, offering both visual and auditory means of learning.

Interactive digital platforms: Utilize platforms like interactive timelines or maps that allow students to explore events and concepts through touch screens or mouse interactions, catering to various sensory preferences and motor abilities.

To accommodate diverse linguistic backgrounds and ensure comprehension of the standard, employ these strategies:

- **Multilingual glossaries:** Create or provide glossaries that explain key terms and concepts in multiple languages, supporting students who are English language learners.
- **Visual aids:** Use charts, diagrams, and infographics to represent the development of colonial governments visually. Symbols and imagery can help bridge language barriers and aid in understanding complex historical concepts.

To support students in building knowledge, consider these methods:

- **Collaborative learning:** Organize group projects where students create presentations or digital stories that connect colonial government developments to revolutionary ideas, encouraging peer-to-peer learning.
- **Storytelling and narratives:** Share stories or narratives from diverse perspectives within the colonial era, including Indigenous people, enslaved Africans, and women. This approach enriches understanding through varied linguistic and cultural lenses.

As you can see above, in seconds, ChatGPT provided numerous approaches to ensure that all students have options for how they learn. These methods enable students to build both individual and collective knowledge, honoring the unique ways they perceive, process, and connect with content.

As with options for support, blended learning can allow you to incorporate more of these means of representation than might seem feasible. So, you may decide to use the whole-group rotation model to offer students a "would you rather" option for the instruction portion of a lesson. You can explain that students can self-pace through an instructional video or join a small-group, teacher-led instructional session. That way, your students can decide whether they prefer to put on their headphones and watch an instructional video, pausing and responding to questions, or take notes while they listen to you present the information live. This provides two possible pathways to access the information.

Some teachers may question why they would invest time in making a video if they are also going to present the information live, but it's important to remember that live instruction presents myriad barriers for some students. The time you invest in creating a video pays dividends, as it can be used to provide repeat instruction. The video can also be a resource when providing feedback since students may need to revisit instruction to revise their work.

We provided ChatGPT with the following prompt to help us design resources for students' strategy development, to support their executive function.

> **Catlin and Katie:** "How can I design activities that help students plan, organize, and manage their proects as they work toward [specific standard]?"

In response, the robot fairies swooped in and suggested that we include activities we've outlined in table 5.3. Again, to emphasize blended learning, we worked with ChatGPT to present these activities as part of a playlist.

> ### *Keyword Alert!*
>
> **Multiple means of action and expression:** Learners vary in how they navigate learning environments, engage with the learning process, and express their understanding. When given an option, some learners may find written assignments more suitable for them, allowing them to organize their thoughts and present complex ideas. Others might excel with oral presentations, where verbal articulation aligns better with desired results. This variability extends to task management: For some, structured environments with clear guidelines and step-by-step instructions are crucial for demonstrating mastery. Others may thrive in open-ended situations that encourage creative exploration, highlighting the importance of aligning task demands with the standards being assessed. Because there is no single method of action and expression for everyone, educators need to design options for interaction, expression and communication, and strategy development.

Multiple Means of Action and Expression

When it comes to action and expression, we have already provided numerous options for students to share their understanding of colonial America through several assessment options. But, given those choices, many students may struggle with executive function. Executive function is crucial for learning, enabling individuals to act skillfully, set goals, and strategize. When examining action and expression, the focus of executive function is on strategy development.

> **Keyword Alert!**
>
> **Executive function:** A set of cognitive processes and mental skills that enable individuals to develop emotional capacity, build knowledge, and create strategies to achieve goals and solve problems. These skills are crucial for planning, organizing, paying attention to and remembering details, and managing time and space.

Table 5.3: Assessment Playlist: Supporting Executive Functioning

Assessment Playlist: Supporting Strategy Development	
Explain Your Choice! • Why did you select a particular type of assessment? • What motivated your choice? Did it appeal to your strengths or interests?	**Options:** Write or record your explanation.
Set a Goal for Yourself Identify a clear, achievable goal for yourself as you work on this project. • What do you want to work toward? • How will you make progress toward this goal? • What will success look or feel like when you achieve this goal?	**Options:** Complete the graphic organizer or record your ideas below.
Support Choice Board Watch or read the resources related to the topic(s) you need more help with, and capture your notes/questions in this column. ☞ • Research techniques • Note-taking strategies • Citations • Assessing website credibility	**Notes:**

Project Planning	**Options:** Provide a link to your project
Select a project planning tool from the list below that you want to use to break down your project into a series of smaller, more manageable tasks. • Trello • Google Keep • Asana Add a timeline to the parts of your project to ensure you can finish and submit it on time.	planning tool or capture a screenshot of your project breakdown to insert below.

Teacher Check-in: Students pause their progress to meet with the teacher to review their project plan.

Peer Feedback	**Options:** Write or record your
Find two other members in the class to provide you with peer feedback. To structure their feedback, ask them to select two prompts from this peer feedback choice board. Once you have received feedback, reflect in this column. ☞	response to peer feedback. • What did you learn about your areas of strength and areas in need of development from this feedback? • How do you plan to incorporate this feedback to improve your product?
Self-Assessment	**Options:** Share the link to your
You're almost done! Use the rubric to assess a draft of your finished product, identifying your level of mastery in relation to each criterion and explaining your assessment score in a brief written or recorded response. Make any last-minute changes necessary.	completed self-assessment or recording here.

Final Reflection	Options: Capture your reflection in writing, a recording, or drawings and include below.
Think about your experience working on this assessment. Select three of the questions below to guide a reflection. • How did this project challenge your understanding of the subject matter? • What strategies did you use to overcome obstacles during this project? Were they effective? • Can you describe a situation during this project where you had to seek out resources to solve a problem? How did you go about finding and utilizing these resources? • What new tools or resources have you learned to use during this project, and how will you apply them in the future? • What planning or organizational strategies did you find most effective during this project? • How did you prioritize tasks and manage your time throughout this project? • Looking back, what would you do differently in planning and executing this project to make it more successful?	

ChatGPT's first iteration of the playlist was a strong start; however, we added elements, like the first stop on the playlist, which asks students to reflect on and explain why they selected the assessment option they chose. We want students to become more aware of the decisions they are making and what is motivating those choices. We also included options for how students could share their thinking—writing or recordings—and the tools they could use to organize their project plan.

Again, AI collaboration makes for a strong start, not an endpoint. Instead of requiring all students to attend workshops on specific skills (since we knew not every student would need the same instruction and support when it came to their research, citation, and note-taking skills), we envisioned the playlist as a support choice board. That way, students could read or watch resources targeting specific areas of need they might encounter during work. If you identify an area of need during check-in, you can also ask students to revisit a specific category of resources to improve the quality of their work. Some of the suggestions, like offering a presentation skills workshop, were not applicable to all students, so we chose not to include them at all.

As students work through the playlists you develop for your own courses, you can run optional skill stations or workshops on topics like presentation or time management skills. That makes it possible for students who need support to access it in a small-group, teacher-led instructional session. Remember, the goal of a playlist like this is to help students develop the skills necessary to plan a multi-step project; monitor their progress; access support in the form of videos, resources, and teacher check-ins; and reflect. All these elements will ultimately help students be more successful in demonstrating their learning.

One-Sentence Summary

UDL and blended learning can help teachers design flexible, inclusive, and equitable learning experiences that accommodate the diverse needs of all students, ensuring every learner can access and engage with rigorous grade-level content.

Reflect and Discuss

1. Considering the concept of UDL as it relates to both physical architecture and educational spaces, analyze the potential impacts of design choices on accessibility and inclusion. Use

the examples from the text, such as the bank and Hunters Point Library, to evaluate how design can either enable or hinder access to learning opportunities for all students.

2. UDL emphasizes the necessity of providing multiple means of engagement, representation, and action and expression to accommodate diverse learner needs. Drawing from your own teaching practice or observations, propose a lesson or activity redesign that aligns with UDL principles and addresses potential barriers you've identified. How would you ensure this redesign is construct-relevant and supports high-level learning outcomes?

3. Think about the goals of blended learning described in this chapter. How can blended learning and the strategic use of both technology and teacher time help to provide multiple means of engagement, representation, and action and expression?

4. How can you leverage blended learning models, like the station rotation and playlist models, to provide students with a more equitable learning experience?

5. Reflect on the statement "UDL isn't a framework you can implement overnight." Discuss the iterative process of integrating UDL principles into teaching and learning. What challenges might educators face in this journey, and how can the strategies of self-assessment, peer support, and continuous feedback play a role in overcoming these challenges? Provide examples of how you or other educators could use these strategies to refine and improve lesson designs for inclusivity and effectiveness.

Time to Apply!

Based on what you learned in this chapter, take a traditional lesson and redesign it using UDL guidelines and AI!

- **Step 1:** Select a lesson to focus on. It can be a lesson you designed or one from your adopted curriculum.

- **Step 2:** Use the prompts in this chapter and AI to generate ideas for how you can provide multiple means of engagement in this lesson to generate interest and maintain effort and persistence.
- **Step 3:** Think about multiple means of representation. Use the questions in this chapter and AI as a thought partner to generate various ways to present information so that it will be accessible for students.
- **Step 4:** Finally, let's incorporate multiple means of action and expression into this lesson. Consider barriers in the current lesson that might make it challenging for students to share their learning. Use AI and blended learning models to generate flexible pathways that allow students multiple avenues to demonstrate their learning. Then use the prompts in this chapter to generate ideas for how to help students with their executive functioning as they work to create an artifact of their learning.

CHAPTER 6

Removing Barriers and Creating Flexible Pathways

Annotations Aren't for Everyone

Catlin   As an English literature major at UCLA, it was not uncommon for me to have over eight hundred pages of reading a week. I loved to read, but that was a lot in addition to attending classes and waiting tables at Jerry's Famous Deli in Westwood. To complicate matters, I'm dyslexic, so reading has always been a slow and methodical process. It takes a concerted effort to track the words on a page and process what I am reading. Early on in my educational career, I discovered that annotations were a critical tool for me. I've always relied heavily on notes or jotting down questions, comments, and key phrases in the margins to aid my comprehension. All my books have underlined words, circled phrases with arrows connecting ideas, and notes in the margin. Annotations are how I leave metaphorical tracks in the snow that help me to digest and remember what I'm reading. This informed my approach to active reading when I became a high school English teacher.

Every night, I required my students to annotate the reading they completed at home. They had to have a minimum of three annotative notes per page to receive full credit for the homework. Spoiler alert! They hated it, and they let me *know* they hated it on the semester feedback form! When asked "What would you like to do less of in this class?" the majority of my students (and I mean more than 90 percent) said "annotations."

Despite this feedback, I was immovable for years. Annotations had been invaluable to me. I figured my students just didn't appreciate them *yet*, and that one day they would come to realize I was right. However, as my approach to teaching shifted, and I began prioritizing student agency and meaningful choice into my blended lessons, I observed how much more interested and engaged my students were in the learning happening in class.

To make a change that could better serve my students, I spent the summer delving into alternative active reading strategies. I read a book about dialogic journals and watched countless YouTube videos about how to draw sketchnotes to process reading. When I returned to campus for the new school year, I decided to try three different active reading strategies, spending two weeks practicing each. After that six-week onboarding, students could decide how they wanted to actively engage with the texts we read.

The impact of this change was immediate and impressive. Not only did more students consistently complete their reading assignments and provide evidence of active reading, but when I collected feedback at the end of that semester, only 2 out of 168 students reported wishing we would do less active reading with texts. I was blown away! Simply allowing students to choose which active reading strategy they wanted to use made all the difference.

As I think back on that experience, I remember the significant time investment required to generate these alternatives for students. Now, in an era of AI, that process would have taken a fraction of the time. For example, when I asked ChatGPT, "What are some examples of strategies secondary students can use to read actively?" the

AI listed ten different strategies students might use to engage deeply with texts, including graphic organizers, interactive note-taking, text-coding, dialogic journals, and comparative analysis. Most of these would not have even occurred to me without such a useful brainstorming partner! In addition to generating meaningful options, AI can also produce step-by-step directions, create scaffolds, and provide exemplars for students to reference as they learn how to employ each active reading strategy.

This experience taught me that there is value in giving students meaningful choices so they can understand what works for them (not me!). Students need opportunities to try different approaches and time to reflect on those choices to understand what helps them to be successful as learners. What I did not realize early in my career was that many of the instructional strategies and tasks I used presented myriad barriers for my students. Annotations were just the tip of the iceberg!

When we work with teachers, we tell them the easiest way to remove barriers in a lesson and ensure diverse groups of learners can be successful is to provide students with agency and meaningful choices. This flexibility not only accommodates diverse learners but also encourages autonomy and self-regulation. When students feel they have a say in what or how they learn, they are more likely to be motivated to actively participate and persist in their learning. By leveraging AI tools, educators can more efficiently generate diverse options and supportive resources for students, ensuring all learners have access to high-quality, tailored educational experiences.

Strong Pedagogical Practices

Student Agency

Humans are naturally gifted with intrinsic motivation (lucky us!). We have an innate curiosity and desire to explore and develop mastery.

Yet research has shown that motivation declines the longer a child is in school.[1] So, the question is not whether students possess intrinsic motivation. They have it! We just have to nurture it. Here are the questions we should be asking:

- How do we tap into our students' innate curiosity?
- How do we position students as active agents in a lesson?
- How can we create the conditions in the classroom that encourage and support the intrinsic motivation that may be buried after years of schooling?
- How and when can we integrate agency and choice to ensure students feel they can be successful completing assignments?

Keyword Alert!

Intrinsic motivation: The desire to engage in an activity for its own sake. Unlike extrinsic motivation, which is fueled by external rewards or pressures (e.g., grades or approval), intrinsic motivation comes from within the individual because they derive personal satisfaction, enjoyment, or a sense of accomplishment from the activity itself. It is characterized by an interest in the task, a desire to explore and learn, and a commitment to personal growth and fulfillment.

When there is only one pathway to acquire information, process that information, or demonstrate learning, students may not feel confident they can be successful. Student agency, or the ability to make key decisions about their learning experience, satisfies two core psychological needs that positively impact self-motivation and overall well-being: autonomy and competence.[2] In an educational setting, autonomy is the degree of control, choice, and independence students have over their learning experiences. This can include decisions about what they learn, how they learn it, when they learn, and how they demonstrate their understanding and mastery of a concept or skill. By contrast, competence refers to a student's confidence in their ability to perform a particular task or master content. In both cases—autonomy and competence—providing students with meaningful choices is critical to creating conditions where their intrinsic motivation is nurtured, not undermined. Research has shown that when students are highly motivated, they are more likely to remain engaged and persist in their learning tasks.[3,4] Moreover, giving students the agency to make significant choices in a lesson honors learner variability, removes barriers, and creates flexible pathways through a learning experience, which is why it is a pillar of best practice in both UDL and blended learning.

The term "voice and choice" is commonly used to signify students' ability to make decisions within the learning environment. However, what students have voice and choice over is critical. In a recent conversation on Catlin's podcast, *The Balance*, James Anderson made the point that not all choice is created equal. He made a distinction between trivial and significant choices.[5] Anderson underscores the importance of offering students opportunities to make challenging decisions, as this helps them transition from a fixed mindset to a growth mindset, positively impacting their confidence in their capabilities. Robert Marzano echoes this sentiment when he says, "To reap [the benefits of learner agency], a teacher should create choices that are robust enough for students to feel that their decision has an impact on their learning."[6] Making important decisions empowers students to perceive themselves as active agents who shape their experiences, rather than passive recipients of their circumstances. However, to make significant decisions with confidence, students need practice, as well as chances to reflect on their choices and their outcomes.

We have worked with countless teachers who report that students respond to choice like deer in the headlights. Other students even seem frustrated when given options. The challenge of exercising agency lies in the reality that many students spend all day in classrooms where they do not get to make any decisions. As a result, the moments when they *are* given choice may feel unfamiliar and uncomfortable. Similarly, teachers may not be used to offering students choices because it is easier, from a logistic perspective, to have all students working on the same task in the same way and producing the same products.

Though uniformity may make it easier for teachers to monitor progress and assess student work, it does not honor learner variability or acknowledge that students do not communicate or express their learning the same way. Instead, we encourage teachers to consider three aspects of a lesson or learning cycle where they should give students meaningful and appropriate choices: content, process, and product. See table 6.1 for more detail.

Table 6.1: Three Opportunities for Student Agency in a Lesson

Content	Process	Product
• Content choices allow students to make decisions about *what* they learn. Students can pursue learning through a lens of interest. • Content choices increase student engagement, confidence, and self-efficacy.	• Process choices invite students to decide *how* they do something. Students decide how to complete a task given their strengths and learning preferences. • Process choices increase students' confidence in their ability to complete the task.	• Product choices give students meaningful options for how they communicate or demonstrate their learning. • Product choices provide students with different ways to express and communicate their learning, boosting their feelings of competence.

• What does the student want to learn? • Is there an aspect of the larger topic they want to learn more about or are particularly interested in? • Can they select the lens they look through as they approach a particular topic or assignment? • Can they select the type of content they want to engage with to learn?	• How does the student want to work? • How will students complete the task? • What steps will they take to complete the task? • What materials or tools will they use? • Will they work offline or online? • How will they track their own progress toward completion?	• What is the purpose of the task, assignment, or project? • Given the purpose, what type of product do students want to create? • How do they want to demonstrate their learning? • What option do they believe will help them to accurately demonstrate their learning?
Example: In a history unit on the American Civil War, students can choose to join an expert group investigation focused on military strategy, the home front, or the role of African American soldiers to learn more about specific aspects of the war they are particularly interested in.	**Example:** In a unit on solving linear equations, students might choose between graphing equations on graph paper for a tactile, hands-on experience or using an online graphing program like Desmos for a more digital, interactive approach.	**Example:** In a science unit focused on renewable energy sources, students can decide to present their argument about the best source of renewable energy in a TED-style talk for the class, an argumentative essay, or a detailed infographic.

AI Integration

The idea of building student agency into a lesson or unit may have felt daunting or time-consuming prior to artificial intelligence, but AI has simplified the process of generating meaningful and appropriate choices. When designing lessons to include student agency, we suggest teachers start small with a "would you rather" approach to meaningful choice. Starting with two choices can help teachers get used to integrating student agency into their lessons without overwhelming students with too many choices, especially in the beginning. That way, students can build their stamina and confidence around decision-making.

To begin incorporating student agency, think about the individual instructional strategies you are using—mini-lessons, whole-class discussion, writing prompts—and consider the barriers that might make it challenging for a student to participate in the activity or complete the task. If you aren't sure what barriers might prevent students from being successful, ask your AI thought partner!

Keyword *Alert!*

Mini-lesson format: A structured approach to teaching that focuses on delivering concise, targeted instruction on a specific skill, concept, or strategy within a short period, typically ten to fifteen minutes. The mini-lesson format is designed to maximize instructional time and maintain student engagement. It often follows a predictable sequence of "I do, we do, you do" for clarity and effectiveness.

We asked ChatGPT, "What might prevent students from acquiring information when I present concepts live in the class using the mini-lesson format?" It generated a long list that included the following items:

- Auditory processing challenges
- Visual impairments
- Cognitive overload
- Language barriers
- Distractions in the environment
- Lack of background knowledge
- Physical and mental fatigue

In addition to these barriers, students may have learning attention challenges or anxiety or trauma issues that make it challenging
to acquire information presented in real time. Realistically, sometimes students are also absent and miss instruction entirely.

So, faced with these barriers, how might we use meaningful
choices to provide flexible pathways to acquiring information? We
asked our AI thought partner to help us generate "would you rather"
choices that teachers could use to give students meaningful input
on how they acquire information, and table 6.2 shows a couple of
options we really liked!

Table 6.2: Would You Rather Options to Acquire Information

Would You Rather?	
Join a teacher-led instructional session	Self-pace through a video lesson
Use the reciprocal teaching strategy to engage in discussion with peers while reading a complex text	Draw sketchnotes and capture golden lines while listening to a podcast

Beyond eliminating barriers, teachers can also explore ways to
empower students with agency over what they learn, how they learn,
and how they demonstrate and communicate their understanding.
AI is a powerful tool for suggesting strategies on that front as well.
The prompts in table 6.3 are designed to help educators generate and
integrate choices related to content, process, and product into their
lessons and units.

Table 6.3: AI Prompts—Giving Students Agency over Content, Process, and Product

AI Prompts: Giving Students Agency Over Content, Process, and Product	
Content	• Generate a list of subtopics within [topic] that students can choose to explore or research to deepen their learning. • What thematic or inquiry-based questions can students choose to guide their exploration of [topic]? • Can you list different types of resources (books, articles, videos, podcasts) that offer diverse perspectives on [topic]? • Identify cross-disciplinary links that students could investigate to enrich their study of [topic]. • What are some real-world problems or scenarios related to [topic] that students could solve or address?
Process	• What different steps or stages can students choose from to progress through [task]? • Can you list various materials or tools that students can choose to use while working on [assignment or task]? • What are some activities related to [topic or task] that students can choose to do online, and what are alternative offline options? • What are some different note-taking strategies that students can select from to help them best retain information from [resource] or about [topic]? • What strategies might you provide to allow students to reflect on their learning? • Can you provide a range of problem-solving techniques that students might apply when facing challenges related to [task, process, or assignment]? • Identify technology tools that students can use for [task or assignment]. • What project management strategies can students select to best organize and tackle [task, assignment, or project]?

Product	• What are some ways students can creatively express what they have learned about [topic]? • Can you suggest a variety of creative project ideas that students can select from to share their learning about [topic, subject, or standard]? • What are some digital tools or platforms that students can use to create interactive presentations or multimedia projects on [topic]? • List different types of written work, such as essays, reports, or journals, that students can choose to articulate their learning of [standard, concept, or skill]. • What alternatives to written assignments can you use to assess students' understanding of [standard, concept, or skill]? • Can you provide ideas for performance-based demonstrations, like role-plays or simulations, that allow students to act out concepts from [topic]? • Identify technology-enhanced project options, like creating websites, blogs, or videos, that students can use to convey their knowledge of [standard, concept, or subject]. • What options, such as leading a workshop or a video tutorial, can you provide students if you want them to teach their peers about [topic]?

As you have probably noticed from our interactions with AI, you will get more suggestions than you need or want. The suggestions will also be of varying quality and accuracy, so it's critical that you evaluate the options provided by AI and select the ones that are best aligned with your curriculum and most likely to appeal to your students.

We also encourage teachers using an adopted curriculum to remember that just because a lesson is written a particular way doesn't mean that is the only way to teach it. If you feel like a particular instructional strategy or activity isn't working well for your students, or you want to add some variety to lessons that use the same structure every day, we encourage you to ask AI about alternatives that target the same standard, skill, concept, or process but gives students agency to choose what will work best for them.

One-Sentence Summary

Providing students with agency and meaningful choices in their learning experiences accommodates diverse needs, nurtures intrinsic motivation, and removes barriers, and educators can leverage AI to generate tailored educational strategies, creating flexible learning pathways.

Reflect and Discuss

1. Reflect on a time when you noticed a barrier that affected a student's ability to learn or engage. What was the barrier, and how did you address it?

2. How can recognizing and removing barriers in the classroom enhance a student's sense of autonomy and competence? Discuss specific examples related to content, process, or product choices.

3. Reflect on the relationship between student choice, motivation, and academic performance. How does empowering students with choices influence learning outcomes?

4. How can teachers balance the need to teach the curriculum while providing meaningful choices that accommodate diverse learning needs and preferences?

5. What challenges might teachers face when trying to implement student choice in the classroom? Discuss ways to overcome these challenges.

Time to Apply!

Let's apply what you learned in this chapter about student agency and meaningful choice.

- **Step 1:** Select an instructional strategy you use frequently (e.g., whole-group discussions, writing assignment) and use an AI chatbot to help you identify all the barriers that might make it challenging for students to successfully participate in the activity or complete the task.

- **Step 2:** Use AI to generate a meaningful "would you rather" choice to provide flexible pathways through the learning experience.
- **Step 3:** Share your "would you rather" choice with a colleague or coach and ask for feedback. Do they have any suggestions for improvement?
- **Step 4:** Think about how you can encourage students to reflect on their choice and how well it worked for them. When might you build this reflective practice into class? What form could this reflection take? How can you provide students with meaningful choices in how they reflect?

PART III

Personalizing Instruction

Design Path

STEP 1
Identify Desired Results
Align Desired Results and Assessment Strategy

STEP 2
Design Equitable Learning Experiences
Universally Designed Blended Learning

STEP 3
Adapt and Personalize Instruction and Support
Use Data Strategically to Identify and Respond to Needs

CHAPTER 7

Personalizing Instruction with Data-Driven Design

Inclusive Practice Family Reunion

Katie   I recently had the opportunity to connect with Carol Ann Tomlinson, *the* mother of differentiated instruction (DI). The goal of our conversation was to better understand the relationship between UDL and DI, as there is so much confusion and overlap that I wanted the definitive answer. After a couple of Zoom calls, we decided that the two frameworks are inclusive practice cousins. We joked that when they were born, they were different, but as they have aged, they have become more and more alike. Dare I say, they might even be ready for a family reunion.

First, I'd like to introduce UDL—the "cool, techy cousin." Picture them wearing virtual reality goggles and hipster jeans, always thinking ahead and designing innovative solutions for every learning challenge before it even arises. UDL's origins are in special education. The framework was developed by the Center for Applied Special Technology (now simply CAST). When UDL emerged, the focus was on including students with disabilities in classrooms with their peers. It leveraged a proactive design process and innovative assistive technology to support all students in accessing grade-level instruction. From the beginning, UDL encouraged educators to shift from identifying student deficits to recognizing design flaws in learning environments.

Differentiated instruction is the "big-picture cousin." Imagine DI sporting a classic blazer and a pair of comfortable, well-worn sneakers, ready to adapt and navigate diverse classroom needs with ease. At its inception, DI recognized that one-size-fits-all classrooms weren't effective for diverse student populations. As the education community moved away from tracking and ability grouping, it became evident that students have varied needs. Teachers can't rely on uniform lessons when students require different levels of challenge and support to achieve the same goals. DI provides educators with a framework to create a balanced, holistic approach to teaching and learning by continuously harmonizing the learning environment, curriculum, assessment, instruction, and classroom routines to respond to learners' needs. DI requires teachers to be flexible and responsive, offering targeted instruction and individualized support when necessary, along with flexible grouping and regrouping to ensure that all learners receive what they need.

So, our inclusive practice cousins came from different "families," but now they are working together in the family business and absolutely *nailing* it. Both frameworks require second-order change—a deep, fundamental transformation of the system and a shift away from one-size-fits-all learning. To create an environment that is proactive, evidence-based, and responsive, we must consistently use data to inform our decisions. This means continuously analyzing student performance and feedback to tailor instruction and interventions. By collaborating with learners to adjust strategies as needed, we ensure that teaching is personalized and adaptive, meeting the unique needs of every student and fostering a culture of continuous improvement and inclusivity.

Throughout the text, we have explored how UDL leverages technology to proactively create inclusive learning environments. In this chapter, we want to examine how AI supports the entire "family," including DI. We already know AI offers diverse resources and flexible options, but it also aids in differentiating instruction by dynamically adjusting strategies, providing targeted support, and enabling flexible grouping. But to do this well, we need to create a strong data culture.

> **Keyword A*lert!***
>
> **Differentiated instruction (DI):** Carol Ann Tomlinson defines differentiated instruction as a teaching approach that tailors learning experiences to meet students' diverse needs. It is "teaching with the children in mind," and it emphasizes that educators should plan and adapt their instruction based on students' readiness, interests, and learning profiles.[1]

Strong Pedagogical Practices

Collecting and using data is key to designing learning experiences with the high level of intentionality that makes them responsive to specific student needs. This intentionality is critical when we are using UDL and blended learning to design equitable learning experiences and create inclusive classroom communities. We must use data to understand 1) where our students are starting in their individual learning journeys, 2) the perspectives, lived experiences, and prior knowledge they possess, and 3) how much progress they are making toward individual learning objectives and the larger desired results of the unit.

Often, when teachers hear the word *data*, they think of the data generated by standardized exams. That isn't the type of data we are discussing in this chapter. Instead, the data cycle we are focused on is the data you collect about your students to better understand their unique needs, skills, and abilities. By collecting data at strategic moments in the design and learning process, we can more effectively ensure that all students have equal access to learning and feel like valued and supported members of an inclusive learning community.

By collecting data at strategic moments in the design and learning process, we can more effectively ensure that all students have equal access to learning and feel like valued and supported members of an inclusive learning community.

Collecting and capitalizing on data are interrelated processes. Accordingly, the goal of the data-driven design cycle in figure 7.1 is to highlight the importance of ongoing assessment in effectively responding to the needs of diverse groups of learners. This cycle helps to ensure the teacher is not only designing for their specific group of students but also continually collecting and responding to data as students progress toward firm, standards-aligned learning goals.

Pre-assessment: Collecting Data to Inform Our Initial Design

Learning is not like lining up for a race shoulder to shoulder. Students do not all begin in the same place when it comes to understanding concepts and applying skills. They have different needs, abilities, language proficiencies, and background knowledge that impact where they begin in their individual learning journeys.

Students also bring a lifetime of experiences, cultural backgrounds, and individual interests into the classroom that may impact what they know and can do. For example, in a history class exploring

Figure 7.1: Data-Driven Design Cycle

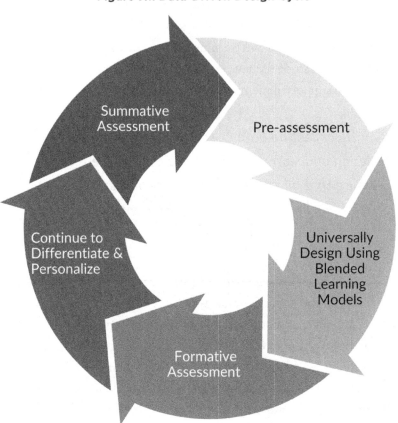

the civil rights movement in the United States, one student might have heard firsthand stories from a grandparent who participated in peaceful protests during the 1960s. In an elementary science discussion about the solar system, another student might contribute insights gained from a book like *The Magic School Bus Lost in the Solar System* by Joanna Cole. A high school English student fluent in Spanish might have a unique advantage with challenging vocabulary words that are cognates, like *amiable* (*amable* in Spanish). These diverse experiences and perspectives can add richness and depth to the learning environment *if* teachers know about them.

As teachers, we can employ a variety of strategies to determine what students know or can do before we begin universally designing blended lessons that are intended to move learners toward a clear desired result. You may simply want to assess prior knowledge, asking students to engage in a quick write, respond to a prompt, or conduct a two-minute chat with a classmate about their knowledge of a topic and how they learned it. In table 7.1, we've curated some of our favorite strategies for encouraging students to access and share their prior knowledge. These strategies can be used offline, with pencil and paper, or with variety of online tools to quickly capture and save student responses.

Table 7.1: Accessing Prior Knowledge Strategies

Strategy	Description
Entrance Ticket	Design a simple entrance ticket to assess what students know or think about a topic. Ask questions that encourage them to do the following: • Share their prior knowledge • Identify aspects of the topic they are interested in or curious about • Explain what they think key vocabulary words mean
Quick Write or Freewrite	Present students with a prompt related to the topic and encourage them to write for a set amount of time (e.g., five minutes). Explain that the goal is not perfect spelling and grammar but rather to write as much as possible in a limited amount of time.
Pre-assessment or Quick Quiz	Design a quick assessment to gauge students' understanding of key concepts or skills at the start of the learning. These scores should not go in a grade book but rather be used to provide the teacher with information about students' prior knowledge.
Online Discussion	Present students with a question or prompt and ask them to share what they know, where they learned it, and what they are wondering about. Encourage students to post replies to their peers after they submit their responses to learn with and from each other.

Two-Minute Talks	Pair students in class or breakout rooms for a quick chat about a topic, concept, or skill. Give each student one minute to share what they know about it. Then, prompt them to switch roles. The teacher can move around the room or pop in and out of breakout rooms to listen and observe. They can also follow the chat by asking students to capture a quick written explanation of what they shared.
Draw What You Know	Ask students to surface their prior knowledge with a drawing (for younger learners) or a sketchnote (for older learners), identifying the central ideas or concepts and visually showing how they relate to one another.
Concept Map	Give students a collection of keywords or vocabulary terms and ask them to create a concept map to show what the words mean and their relationship to one another.

When educators take time to identify and understand where students are beginning their learning in relation to key ideas and skills, they can universally design blended lessons to ensure every student gets what they need to navigate the learning experience.

An experience during a coaching session with a high school science teacher reinforced the importance of pre-assessment for Catlin. The teacher was planning a unit about possible solutions to climate change. Catlin asked her if the class had already learned about climate change and its causes. The teacher explained that it was covered in the grade before. Catlin suggested that they design a pre-assessment to understand what students actually knew about climate change and its causes before diving into a unit focused on solutions. The duo gave students class time to define climate change in their own words and list or create a concept map of the causes. This pre-assessment revealed that about 20 percent of the class could not accurately define climate change or list the causes, 35 percent could provide a partial definition and list at least one cause, and 25 percent could define it accurately and list one or two causes. Just 20 percent of the class clearly and accurately defined climate change and listed three or more causes.

Given this data, it was clear the teacher needed to provide differentiated instruction and support to the 20 percent of students who could not define climate change or list any causes and the 35 percent who could only provide a partial definition and one cause. To create the time and space to work with these students, she had the 20 percent who could define climate change and list multiple causes collaborate to create a review and practice choice board for the unit they had just completed. The goal was for them to engage their higher-order thinking to generate questions and activities that could be used for review in the future. The 25 percent of the class that was able to define climate change but only list one or two causes used the reciprocal teaching strategy we discussed in our book *The Shift to Student-Led*. So, they listened to and then discussed a podcast on the causes of climate change, stopping at regular intervals to engage in a conversation. The overall goal was to ensure each group was engaged in a learning activity designed to help provide a firm foundation for the unit.

Without pre-assessment data, it is easy to make assumptions about what students know or can do and design learning experiences that either repeat content students already know or present new content that students do not have the background knowledge, vocabulary, or skill set to access. Either way, the result is students who are either bored or lost, making them more likely to disengage.

Formative Assessment: Collecting Data During a Lesson

When teachers plan a lesson, they are often focused on what students will learn. We want teachers to also consider this question: "What will I learn about my students in this lesson?" That's where formative assessment is incredibly helpful! Formative assessment data is what we collect to understand how much progress students are making toward individual lesson objectives on their path toward the unit's desired results.

Formative assessment is an ongoing process that collects evidence of student learning from both informal and formal methods. It provides information to both the teacher and the student, and it involves two-way communication between the student and teacher. It encourages teachers to continually modify and adjust their instruction and support to meet the needs of the students in their class. Not only is formative assessment a powerful tool for teachers, but it should also serve as a metacognitive tool for students, encouraging them to set goals, engage in self-assessment, and reflect on their learning.[2]

The goal of formative assessment is to help the teacher and learner better understand their current conceptual knowledge and skill set. Formative assessment strategies should focus on trying to identify areas of strength, gaps in understanding, and misconceptions. This helps teachers and students to focus their time and energy on specific areas in need of development. Much like pre-assessment highlights where students are *beginning* in their learning journeys, formative assessment provides key insights into how they are *progressing*, which is critical if we are striving to be responsive in our approach to instruction.

There are a variety of ways to embed formative assessment strategies into each lesson to collect data and measure student progress. Observational assessment allows teachers to watch, listen, and make notes about what they are observing as students work. This strategy is ideal for deepening our understanding of student behaviors, interactions, and skills. Our observations provide valuable qualitative data, or descriptive and non-numeric data, that complements quantitative assessments (like quizzes) that produce numerical data. As part of the observational assessment, teachers may ask students to engage in a four-corner conversation about a concept or issue.

For this, a small group of students holds a discussion in each of the four corners of the room. Teachers can observe the conversations to determine what students are understanding and where the teacher might need to spend some additional time providing instruction. Techniques such as anecdotal records, checklists, rating scales, and single-point rubrics also allow educators to capture insights into students' progress, engagement, and learning preferences as they observe them interacting with content, tasks, and each other.

Formative assessment may also focus on checking for understanding to gauge how effective a lesson has been at helping students grasp an idea or process. Checking for understanding aims to assess students' comprehension, identify misconceptions, and measure progress toward learning objectives. Quick checks like quizzes, exit tickets, and questioning techniques provide valuable insights. Table 7.2 provides a collection of strategies you can draw from to gather formative assessment data.

Table 7.2: Formative Assessment Strategies

Strategy	Description
Quick Polls	Integrate quick polls into your lessons or playlist to collect data from students. Teachers can use polls to gauge understanding, identify misconceptions or gaps, and check in with students.
Tell Me How Video	Ask students to record a video that does the following: • Explains how they solved a problem • Describes the strategies they used to complete a task • Summarizes the main ideas from a chapter in a textbook • Makes predictions about what they expect to happen in a lab or a novel • Identifies a new vocabulary word and explains it to their peers • Reflects on what they understand as well as what is confusing about a topic, text, or task
Create an Analogy	Ask students to make a comparison or create an analogy. This challenges students to think about a thing's qualities or characteristics to explain how it is similar to something else.

Error Analysis	Generate a series of problems or a sample of work that contains errors. (AI is great for generating these!) Ask students to find the mistakes, correct them, and explain (in writing or verbally in a video recording) how they knew the errors were present and how they went about fixing them.
Quick Quiz	Create a quick assessment to determine what students understand or can do. Consider asking questions about the following: • Key concepts or ideas • Vocabulary • Specific skills • Formulas or processes
Write or Record a Summary	Challenge students to identify the main ideas in a lesson, video, article, chapter of a text, or podcast and write or record a summary identifying and describing those key ideas or main points.
Rate Your Understanding	Check in with students and ask them to evaluate their understanding of key concepts, processes, formulas, vocabulary, or skills. Teachers of younger learners can use an emoji scale, like the ones available in Pear Deck. Teachers of older learners may want to use a form and ask students to explain why they gave themselves a particular rating.

Ultimately, the goal is to have a clear picture of where each student is so that we can be responsive to their needs as they traverse a lesson or sequence of lessons.

Differentiation

As the "big-picture cousin" in our inclusive practice family, DI recognizes that no two students start at the same point or learn in the same way. It's about understanding each student's unique needs and tailoring instruction to ensure everyone has a path to success. Being responsive and adaptive begins with data. Just as our pre-assessments and formative assessments help us understand where students are starting and how they're progressing, they also guide how we differentiate. By knowing where each student is on their learning journey, teachers can design lessons that offer various entry points, paths, and outcomes. DI is about being responsive—adjusting pacing for those who need more time, offering advanced challenges for those ready to push further, and using technology to give personalized feedback and resources. AI can help us to do just that.

AI Integration

In inclusive classrooms, teachers use feedback from formative assessments to create groups of students. So, after reviewing the results of universally designed assessments, you will often find there are three categories of students:[3]

- Students who have fully mastered the content and/or skill and are ready to advance to more challenging tasks or explore additional complex materials
- Students who have a basic understanding of the content and/or skill
- Students who do not yet understand the content and/or skill

In a universally designed classroom, these different groups of students have access to firm goals and flexible means, but their outcomes are not the same. To accelerate learning, teachers need to create small groups of students to provide additional instruction or support. This is where differentiated instruction comes in, and it's where AI can serve as a powerful ally. Review the prompts in table 7.3 and consider how you can use them to create small groups for targeted instruction.

Table: 7.3 ChatGPT Prompts for Generating Small-Group Instructional Ideas

Student Group	ChatGPT Input Prompts
Students who have fully mastered the content and/or skill	• Generate ideas for a project that allows students who have mastered [standard] to explore more complex applications. • Suggest ways I can use peer teaching for students who have excelled in [standard], including possible topics they could teach and methods. • Create a challenge activity related to [standard] that involves higher-order thinking skills like analysis and evaluation. • Design a role-play or simulation exercise that incorporates [standard] into real-world scenarios. What roles and situations could be included?
Students who have a basic understanding of the content and/or skill	• List interactive activities that reinforce [standard] for students with a basic understanding. Include materials and setup instructions. • Provide a plan for a workshop or series of activities on [standard] that can help solidify core concepts through practical application. • What are some effective peer collaboration exercises for [standard] that I can facilitate? Describe the grouping and roles. • Suggest engaging, tech-enabled practices for [standard] that can help students practice and retain core concepts at their own pace.
Students who do not yet understand the content and/or skill	• Develop a set of activities for building foundational skills in [standard]. Include hands-on activities and visual aids. • Outline a structured program for [standard] that starts with basic concepts and progresses incrementally. What are key milestones? • Describe a multi-sensory approach to teach [standard] to students struggling with basic concepts. Include types of sensory inputs. • Generate ideas for small, intensive tutorial sessions on [topic] focusing on foundational concepts. What teaching aids should I use?

To see how these prompts would play out as part of an on-the-ground learning experience, we entered them and used a middle school physical education standard: "Demonstrate effective techniques related to developing muscular strength and endurance, including appropriate and safe use of exercise machines, free weights, and bodyweight exercises." In this scenario, imagine that the PE teacher has already provided safety instruction, asked students to set personalized goals, and paid close attention to each student's technique to provide immediate feedback and corrections.

After three class periods of universally designed instruction, the teacher transitions to a station rotation, pictured in figure 7.2, to provide teacher-led instruction in the weight room. Using AI prompts from previous chapters, the teacher decides on three stations, all of which address the physical fitness and activity standards. Each station lasts approximately fifteen minutes, allowing all students to rotate through each station during a typical class period.

Figure 7.2: Physical Education Station Rotation Lesson

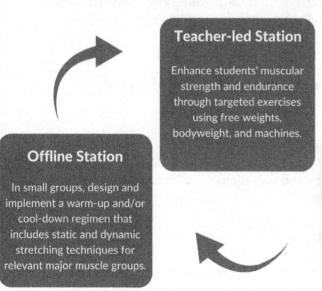

Teacher-led Station

Enhance students' muscular strength and endurance through targeted exercises using free weights, bodyweight, and machines.

Offline Station

In small groups, design and implement a warm-up and/or cool-down regimen that includes static and dynamic stretching techniques for relevant major muscle groups.

Online Station

Students complete a fitness goal reflection, analyzing areas of strength related to physical activity and areas for improvement and post their reflection in their online fitness log using text, audio, or video.

In the scenario pictured in figure 7.2, the online and offline stations are the same for all groups, but the teacher-led station will be differentiated based on student data. ChatGPT provided us with several ideas for each group, and we chose the following to highlight how technology can help us plan targeted instruction based on formative assessment data to ensure that our classrooms are both universally designed and provide targeted instruction.

Students who have fully mastered the content or skill:

ChatGPT: In this advanced session, students will focus on enhancing their strength and endurance through a mini-circuit training setup that incorporates a variety of equipment including free weights, exercise machines, and complex bodyweight exercises. The session will include instruction on advanced techniques such as the proper form for Olympic lifting and methods for safely increasing weight loads. Additionally, a safety and spotting workshop will be integrated into the routine to teach and reinforce spotting techniques, ensuring safety and proper form during weightlifting to prevent injuries and optimize training efficacy.

Students who have a basic understanding of the content and/or skill

ChatGPT: In this session, students will engage in a balanced training regimen that enhances their muscular strength and endurance through a combination of machine, manual, and bodyweight exercises. A concise routine will be developed to include the use of exercise machines, free weights, and essential bodyweight movements. Throughout the session, special emphasis will be placed on form and technique correction to prevent injuries and maximize the effectiveness of the workouts, ensuring that students achieve the best possible outcomes from their training efforts.

Students who do not yet understand the content and/or skill

ChatGPT: In this session, students will be introduced to basic exercises designed to build foundational strength and endurance, emphasizing the use of lighter weights and simpler movements to ensure both understanding and safety. The session will begin with a thorough safety review, reorienting students to the gym equipment and focusing on the correct and safe use of machines and weights. Mini-workshops will follow, concentrating on proper form, breathing techniques, and safe practices, with a particular emphasis on correcting form and technique to prevent injuries and enhance workout effectiveness. Students will use light dumbbells for basic movements such as arm curls, and exercise machines will be set to light settings for exercises like leg extensions and back extensions.

Now, you may be reading this example and think, *Well, of course this sounds like best practice, but I don't have three distinct places where students can work under my supervision.* We absolutely know that every school is different and not all schools have weight rooms that are adjacent to a gymnasium and would allow a teacher to oversee all three groups. But this is where human creativity rules supreme. Instead of thinking of all the reasons a station rotation like this will not work, consider the possibilities. For example, creative solutions may include using underutilized spaces such as the back of the library. Imagine how much more fabulous the online station would be if the library media specialist were able to share tools that support students' fitness goals. Also, think about how community involvement can enhance station rotation models. Consider enlisting family volunteers, local athletes, or high school coaches to facilitate warm-up/cool-down sessions, bringing expertise and additional supervision to the activities. With a bit of creativity and resourcefulness, the station rotation model can be adapted to fit almost any environment!

One-Sentence Summary

By leveraging DI and AI, educators can personalize learning to create inclusive environments that dynamically respond to diverse student needs, ensuring each learner receives the necessary challenges and support to succeed.

Reflect and Discuss

1. Evaluate a situation where you had to adapt your instruction based on formative assessment data. What changes did you make, and how did these adjustments affect student outcomes?

2. Reflect on the long-term impacts of continuous data use in instructional design. How does this practice support equitable learning opportunities, and what are the implications for student engagement and achievement?

3. Given barriers like limited space or resources, discuss innovative station rotation strategies you could employ in your content area.

Time to Apply!

Let's apply what you learned in this chapter about using data to differentiate learning to meet the needs of all students.

- **Step 1:** Identify a standard you're working on. Using one of the formative assessment strategies in table 7.2, determine where your students currently stand in relation to the standards.
- **Step 2:** After reviewing the formative assessment data, categorize students into three groups: those who have mastered the content, those with a basic understanding, and those who haven't mastered the content yet.
- **Step 3:** Use the AI chatbot of your choice (feel free to borrow our good friend ChatGPT!) to generate a first draft of activities for a teacher-led station tailored to each group's

needs. Consider the specific content and/or skills each group should focus on, and design activities that not only reinforce their existing knowledge but also help them work to their fullest potential.

- **Step 4:** Once you have your differentiated teacher-led station ready to go, use AI to help you design online and offline stations that help students engage deeply with concepts and skills in your current unit. Can you give them an opportunity to revisit key concepts and explore their connection to each other? Can learners practice applying a skill, strategy, or process? Can you challenge them to take what they have already learned and apply it to a new situation with peer support?

PART IV

Building Resilience

Design Path

STEP 1
Identify Desired Results
Align Desired Results and Assessment Strategy

STEP 2
Design Equitable Learning Experiences
Universally Designed Blended Learning

STEP 3
Adapt and Personalize Instruction and Support
Use Data Strategically to Identify and Respond to Needs

STEP 4
Cultivate Resilient Learners
Self-Awareness, Perseverance, Adaptability, and Strong
Relationships and Social Support

CHAPTER 8

Cultivating Resilient Learners

The Fire Didn't Destroy Everything

Catlin I started my doctoral journey at Pepperdine University in August of 2017. Two months later, my family lost our home in a wildfire. I remember after the fire, my qualitative research professor called to check on me and tell me that I could press pause on my studies for the year and join the next cohort in 2018. I thanked her for calling, updated her on my situation, and declined the offer to defer my coursework to the following year. I had already waited years to pursue my doctorate, plus I had bonded with the other members of my cohort and did not want to lose those connections and be a year behind them. I wanted to see this through with the impressive and eclectic collection of individuals who were my classmates.

I resented the fire. Not just for all the sentimental items that were destroyed—the little outfits my newborn babies wore home from the hospital, photo albums of relatives long gone, and the pair of bell bottoms I had purchased in London in 1999 while backpacking through Europe with my best friend. All gone. I mourned it all and was determined not to let the fire take anything else from me, including my doctoral journey.

Here is what I knew about myself in the moment I decided to continue with my studies. First, I am highly motivated, goal oriented, and more than a little stubborn. Second, I am a hard worker who is not afraid of a challenge. If I wanted something badly enough, I found a way to make it happen. The program would be hard, but I knew I could do it. Third, I was lucky that I had a strong support system. My parents and my husband's family made countless trips to our rental home to help out with the kids—making meals, driving them to school, and reading endless books before bed. Because of this, I could make the week-long trip to the Pepperdine campus once each month for in-person classes. It was definitely one of those "it takes a village" scenarios. I've never been very good at asking for or accepting help, but I knew I could not do this without it. The strong relationships with my family and friends and the social support we received from our community made it possible for me to juggle it all.

In the two and a half years it took to rebuild our home, I completed my coursework and started my doctoral research. I think back on those years now and I'm not quite sure how I managed it all. Even for me, it was ambitious. I credit my resilience for my ability to bounce back from the fire and pursue a dream I'd had for years. Resilience isn't something we are just born with; it is a skill that develops over time as we weather life's ups and downs. Like many people, I have encountered challenging situations in my life. I believe it is my keen awareness of myself and my circumstances, combined with my strengths, weaknesses, limitations, perseverance, adaptability, strong relationships, and support network that have buoyed me through the most daunting, scary, and overwhelming moments in my life.

When I reflect on the impact we have as educators, I believe helping learners cultivate resilience is the best gift we can give them. Our students may not remember important dates from history, and they may forget how to write a thesis or solve a math problem. But if we help them develop the qualities necessary to face the challenges of life with confidence in themselves, we have given them a foundation that will serve them throughout their lives. By developing and nurturing resilience, we equip our students not just with academic knowledge but with the emotional and psychological tools to navigate whatever trials they may face. This is the true essence of education—not merely to inform, but to empower.

Strong Pedagogical Practices

The word *resilient* comes from the Latin verb *resilire*, meaning to leap or jump back. In her resilience research, Emmy Werner describes "the phenomenon of resilience" as "the dynamic process that leads to positive adaptation within the context of significant adversity."[1] When we use *resilient* to describe a person, we are referring to their ability to rebound after a setback or withstand a difficult situation.

The ability to bounce back is especially important in the context of education. In their most recent guidelines, CAST phased out the phrase "expert learner" because it suggests exclusivity and finite learning. This fails to honor the lifelong accumulation of knowledge, and it overlooks the inherent brilliance in every learner. As educators, we are shifting toward emphasizing ongoing and reflective learning processes. Given this transition, we needed language that speaks to the importance of developing not just accessible, inclusive, and equitable learning experiences, but learners capable of navigating complex education environments with confidence and tenacity. That is why we have chosen the phrase "resilient learners" to describe the students we want to cultivate in our classrooms.

Resilience matters because learning is all about overcoming difficulties. When students enter a classroom at the start of a semester or school year, they are presented with new concepts and skills, diverse peer groups, and sometimes intimidating expectations. Each of these elements poses distinct challenges that can either hinder a student's progress or serve as stepping-stones to greater under-standing and skills. Whether these challenges result in stagnation or growth depends on the student, which is why resilience is crucial. Resilience empowers students to embrace uncertainty, learn from their mistakes, and persist through academic and social pressures. By cultivating resilience in our students, we can help them transform obstacles into opportunities for growth, ensuring they not only sur-vive, but they also thrive.

Beyond the classroom, resilience can also help young people cope with the myriad mental and emotional challenges they face transitioning from childhood to adolescence. As a country, we are experiencing alarming rates of anxiety and depression in young people. These trends began before COVID but have continued to worsen since the pandemic. A whopping 15.08 percent of young people reported experiencing a major depressive episode in the last year.[2] The skyrocketing rates of mental health conditions in young people indicate that many are feeling incapable of managing all the stress and demands in their lives. Our work in the classroom cannot fix the mental health crisis in this country, but it should strive to equip students with the skills to more effectively navigate challenges in school and in life.

The goal of school is not simply to teach students concepts and skills related to a particular subject area; it is also to prepare them for life beyond school. Yet research has shown that teachers are primar-ily focused on content and not necessarily on teaching the critical life skills that will help students navigate the challenges and oppor-tunities they encounter outside the classroom.[3] That is why we have included a focus on the learner in the final step of our AI-enhanced design framework. That student-centered approach emphasizes the reality that helping learners to develop as people is a critical part of education in today's rapidly changing world. Schools must become environments where students not only acquire knowledge but also build the emotional and social tools needed to apply their knowledge creatively and flexibly in real-life situations.

Resilience is not a fixed trait that people either possess or do not possess. It is a trait we can nurture in ourselves and cultivate in others. The National Scientific Council on the Developing Child notes "the essence of resilience is a positive, adaptive response in the face of significant adversity. It is neither an immutable trait nor a resource that can be used up. [Simply put], resilience is rooted in both the physiology of adaptation and the experiences we provide for children that either promote or limit its development."[4] Since kids spend most of their weekdays in school, we have an opportunity to help them develop their resilience each day in classrooms.

Resilience yields numerous and varied benefits, in and out of the classroom. In their book *The Resilience Factor: 7 Keys to Finding Your Inner Strength and Overcoming Life's Hurdles*, Karen Reivich and Andrew Shatté explore the concept of resilience and explain that it is not a fixed trait but rather a continuum, meaning people can learn how to become more resilient over time. Reivich and Shatté write,

> The most resilient people seek out new and challenging experiences because they have learned that it's only through struggle, through pushing themselves to their limits, that they will expand their horizons. Resilient people are able to derive meaning from failure, and they use this knowledge to climb higher than they otherwise would. Resilient people have found a system—and it is a system—for galvanizing themselves and tackling problems thoughtfully, thoroughly, and energetically. Resilient people, like all of us, feel anxious and have doubts, but they have learned how to stop their anxiety and doubts from overwhelming them.[5]

Resilience also aids emotional regulation. With almost 75 percent of high school students reporting negative feelings (including stress) about school, it's clear we need to help learners develop strategies to manage the demands of school in a healthy way.[6] Resilience also fosters adaptability, enabling students to thrive in new environments and adjust to different academic and social settings, maintaining motivation. Beyond these benefits, resilience has been found to yield increased social competence, as well as long-term well-being and improved mental health.

Profile of a Resilient Learner

To design lessons and create classroom cultures that cultivate resilient learners, we must understand the qualities that resilient people possess. We'll focus on four main qualities that resilient people have: self-awareness, perseverance, adaptability, and strong relationships that provide support. See figure 8.1.

Figure 8.1: Qualities of a Resilient Learner

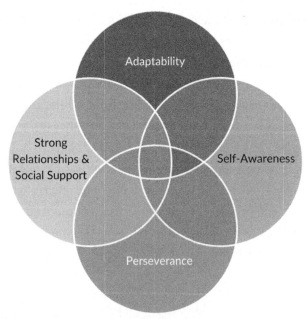

Self-Awareness

Self-awareness is a fundamental skill that involves understanding our emotions, thoughts, and values, and we must recognize how these factors influence our behaviors in different contexts. Self-awareness is a cornerstone of social-emotional learning; without it, students struggle to manage themselves, make responsible decisions, build healthy relationships, and understand and empathize with others.

Self-awareness enables us to merge our personal and social identities, allowing us to appreciate our cultural, linguistic, and personal strengths. It also involves identifying and managing our complex and changing emotions effectively, maintaining honesty and integrity and making meaningful connections between our feelings, values, thoughts, and behaviors. Self-awareness also encourages us to examine prejudices and biases so we can embrace a growth mindset. Developing all these capabilities helps us adapt and cope with challenging situations.

To help cultivate self-awareness in classrooms, educators should consider the following questions:

- How do I model self-awareness in the classroom for my students?
- What routines can help students to identify their emotional state to better understand themselves?
- How can I help students reflect on the connection between their feelings, thoughts, values, and behaviors?
- What classroom routines can help students to develop higher levels of self-efficacy and confidence?
- How can I help students to identify and utilize their personal, cultural, and linguistic assets?

Developing self-awareness must be woven into the fabric of learning. Teachers can use the strategies in table 8.1 to help students identify and understand their emotions, thoughts, and values so they can recognize how these influence their behavior.

Table 8.1: Strategies to Develop Self-Awareness

Strategies to Develop Self-Awareness	
Mood Check-Ins	• Students enter the classroom each day in a particular mood. Maybe they are happy, sad, distracted, or frustrated. Giving them space to identify and share that mood can make for a more productive class for everyone. • Start the class with a mood check-in. Ask students to use a mood meter or emoji scale to assess how they are feeling. The goal is for students to take a moment to check in with themselves. How would they describe their mood today? Who or what is impacting their mood?
Feelings Graph	Tracking feelings helps students identify trends and understand the factors influencing their emotions, enabling them to make more informed decisions. Encourage students to take a few quiet moments to inventory their physical, mental, and emotional states. • Are they tired, stressed, happy, hopeful, or frustrated? • What is causing them to feel this way today? • Did something happen that impacted them positively or negatively? After students assess their feelings, have them chart their emotions on graph paper and write a brief reflection on those chart positions. By monitoring their emotions over time, students can recognize patterns and understand how various factors—like people, routines, and situations—affect their physical, mental, and emotional well-being.

Mindfulness and Stress Management Strategies	Our students' days are a flurry of activity. They are juggling a lot, which is why it is important to provide them with strategies to navigate the demands of their academic and personal lives. Integrate short mindfulness exercises or stress management techniques into your transitions. Breathing exercises, gentle stretches, body scans, short meditations, and journaling prompts can all help students stay calm and grounded in class when shifting from one learning activity to another. • Explain why each technique you use is valuable so students understand the purpose. • Onboard the class to the specific strategies and techniques you want to use. • Consider giving students a choice of which technique to select when they have a few moments to engage in a mindfulness or stress management strategy.
Strengths and Weaknesses Inventory	No one is good at everything. Helping students to identify their strengths and limitations is critical so they can better direct their time and energy. Encourage students to pause after activities, assignments, and tasks to engage in a moment of self-reflection.
STOP Skill + Role-Play	Role-play asks students to assume the identity of a person in a situation that mirrors what they might encounter in the classroom or in life. The scenario might challenge them to think about how they would react if a classmate made a rude comment, they received a low score on an important assignment, or they had to work in a group with a student they did not like. As students engage in a role-play scenario, encourage them to practice the mindfulness STOP skill: **S**top or pause before responding or reacting. **T**ake a deep breath and become aware of their breathing. **O**bserve what is happening inside their bodies and what is happening around them. **P**roceed mindfully based on the information they learn from checking in with themselves and taking a moment to observe the situation.

Perseverance

When students believe in the power of effort, they are more likely to push through setbacks. Perseverance enables us to maintain our effort and focus when we encounter challenges, building character and improving self-discipline. Angela Duckworth's book *Grit: The Power of Passion and Perseverance* explores the role of perseverance and passion in achieving long-term goals and predicting future success.[7] Perseverance also appears in Carol Dweck's research on growth mindset.[8] Dweck emphasizes that the belief in our ability to develop through hard work and determination can positively impact our perseverance.

In an educational setting where students are presented with novel information and tasks daily, perseverance is critical to staying engaged in the learning experience. Perseverance helps students overcome obstacles, persist through lengthy or cognitively challenging assignments, strive for mastery rather than superficial understanding, and achieve deeper learning. When we push through challenges and struggles to complete a task or accomplish a goal, we enjoy greater self-confidence and a more positive outlook on life.

To help cultivate perseverance in classrooms, educators should reflect on the following questions:

- How do I model perseverance for my students?
- How do I react to students' failures? Do I encourage them to reflect and try again?
- Do I proactively teach strategies to help my students respond to and manage challenging or frustrating moments?
- How do I support students in setting and monitoring their progress toward their goals?
- How do I celebrate effort and growth, not just academic success?
- Do I place value on the process of learning?

Table 8.2 offers a collection of strategies teachers can use to help students develop perseverance.

Table 8.2: Strategies to Develop Perseverance

Strategies to Develop Perseverance	
Academic, Behavioral, and Personal Goal-Setting	Goal-setting can have a powerful impact on our students' motivation to push through challenges. It can help them understand how their actions, choices, and behaviors are moving them closer to or farther from things they want to accomplish. Teachers can start the week by asking students to articulate one short-term goal for the week or to set three goals for a grading period or semester. This will frame and focus their work. Use these questions to guide students in thinking deeply about their goals: • What do you want to work toward? • Why is this goal important to you? • How will you make progress toward your goal(s)? • What will you specifically do?
Growth Over Time Analysis and Reflection	To help students appreciate how their hard work is impacting their skills and concept knowledge, ask them to select two similar assignments from two points in the school year and consider the following questions: • What do you notice about the changes in your work? • How have your skills changed and developed? • Where is your growth as a learner most evident? • What do you think contributed most to your growth this year? • What does comparing these two pieces of work reveal about you as a learner?

Problem-Solving Challenges	• Too often students are given solutions to problems they have never encountered. It is important to give them opportunities to struggle productively, building stamina by engaging with unfamiliar and complex problems. • Incorporate challenges that require perseverance, such as puzzles, complex projects, or research tasks that don't have easy or immediate answers. Encouraging students to work together in these moments aids communication, collaboration, critical thinking, and creative problem-solving.
Teacher and Peer Feedback	Provide students with ongoing feedback that emphasizes the process and their effort, helping them identify strengths and areas for improvement. Effective feedback encourages students to refine their work before final submission. When supported by teachers and peers during this process, students are more engaged and better able to navigate challenges. To maximize the impact of feedback, it's crucial to have a structured approach. Encourage students to reflect on specific questions such as these: • What are they working toward? What is the objective of this assignment? • How are they getting there? What strategies are they using? • What are they learning about themselves from the feedback they receive? • Where are they going next? • How are they planning to act on the feedback they receive?
Regular Reflective Practices	• Reflection is a powerful vehicle that helps students think about their progress, contemplate their choices, troubleshoot challenges, identify strategies that are working for them, and analyze the impact of challenges on them. • To remove barriers that might limit the depth of reflection, teachers can provide students with a choice board of reflective prompts and/or different ways of capturing their reflections (e.g., written piece, audio recording, drawing, or chat with classmates).

Adaptability

Adaptability is the capacity to adjust our thoughts, behaviors, and actions in response to new information, changing conditions, or unexpected obstacles. For students, developing adaptability is crucial both for academic success and personal growth, and it allows them to appreciate their growth in the context of the complexities and ever-changing demands of their school and personal lives.[9]

Adaptability offers significant academic benefits. Students who are adaptable excel in modifying and adjusting the strategies they use to meet the demands of different tasks, which enhances their problem-solving skills and encourages creative thinking. Given the variety of learning modalities, instructional strategies, teaching styles, learning tasks, and technology tools that students encounter in school, it is critical that they possess adaptability.

In a study of 2,731 high school students, Andrew J. Martin and colleagues tested a new adaptability scale and found that adaptability is linked to personality traits, beliefs about one's abilities, resilience in the face of daily challenges, and psychological and educational well-being indicators like academic achievement, enjoyment of school, finding meaning and purpose, and overall life satisfaction.[10]

To help cultivate adaptability in classrooms, educators should think about the following questions:

- How do I model adaptability for my students?
- How do I introduce new routines and strategies, etc., in my class? How do I support my students in navigating these changes?
- What opportunities do I provide for students to make choices?
- How do I support students when they face new challenges?
- How can feedback help to foster adaptability? How frequently do I provide students with feedback?

- What role does reflection play in my class? How often do I dedicate class time to reflective practices?

Adaptability can feel abstract, so you can use the concrete strategies in table 8.3 to help students develop this quality.

Table 8.3: Strategies to Develop Adaptability

Strategies to Develop Adaptability	
Diverse Learning Experiences	Introduce students to a diverse array of learning activities and instructional tasks. By blending online and offline experiences, and by alternating between individual and collaborative projects, you can encourage students to adapt their strategies and approaches effectively. Offering varied learning activities not only enhances engagement but also equips students with the flexibility to navigate different learning environments.
Scenario-Based Learning	Scenario-based learning is an instructional strategy that uses realistic situations or challenges to engage students in active problem-solving and decision-making. This method places students in simulations or hypothetical scenarios that mimic real-world contexts, requiring them to apply their knowledge and skills in a practical and often complex setting. Here's how you can apply this approach: • Create scenarios that are closely aligned with the learning objectives and reflect real-life challenges relevant to the subject matter. • Assign roles to students that fit the scenario context. These roles should encourage engagement and require students to adopt perspectives or responsibilities that they might encounter outside of the classroom. • Encourage students to work in teams to discuss and resolve the scenario.
Choice Boards	Offer students choice boards for assignments or projects. These boards should have varied tasks and allow students to choose how they will meet the learning objectives or complete tasks, encouraging them to adapt their methods to their strengths, preferences, and interests.

Collaborative Tasks in Diverse Groupings	Collaborative tasks and group projects require students to adapt to diverse personalities, perspectives, and preferences. These activities necessitate effective listening, equitable task division, clear communication, and compromise. Developing these skills enhances social adaptability, which is essential for success in team-based environments. By navigating these dynamics, students build the interpersonal skills necessary for collaboration and problem-solving in real-world settings.
Small-Group, Student-Led Discussion	Small, student-led group discussions empower learners to engage with a range of ideas and diverse perspectives. These sessions require students to actively listen, respond thoughtfully, and practice communicating their ideas clearly.
	In a discussion, students must learn to analyze, integrate, and synthesize diverse viewpoints, fostering cognitive flexibility. In addition, the task of managing the flow of discussion and ensuring equitable participation further develops their leadership and facilitation skills. These experiences make students more adaptable in any conversational or communicative task, preparing them for complex social interactions and collaborative problem-solving.

Strong Relationships and Social Support

Supportive relationships with peers, teachers, and family members provide students with a vital resource for navigating the challenges of academic life and personal development.[11] Developing these strong connections with people who elicit trust, encourage autonomy, and celebrate initiative helps develop resilience among young people.[12] Strong relationships provide social support, reduce loneliness, and act as buffers against stress, all while helping students develop critical life skills like communication, empathy, and conflict resolution.

The design and facilitation of learning experiences is enhanced when we prioritize human connection and strive to build strong relationships with and among students. Research indicates that strong, positive relationships with peers play a significant role in the social and academic development of children and adolescents. The formation and upkeep of friendships impact a variety of important outcomes, including perceived competence, self-esteem, and academic performance.[13] Given the importance of peer-to-peer relationships at school, it is critical that we center the cultivation of these social connections in our classes, providing students with opportunities to get to know one another and engage in meaningful work together.

As we utilize technology in classrooms, part of the goal should be to free teachers from the front of the room so they can provide more individualized attention, working alongside students to support progress toward standards-aligned learning objectives. One byproduct of a more personalized learning environment is that teachers can build stronger relationships with their students.

To help cultivate stronger relationships and social support in classrooms, consider the following questions:

- How do I build and maintain a sense of community within my classroom?
- What strategies do I use to encourage positive interactions among students?
- How do I manage conflict among my students?
- How often do I design lessons that provide me with opportunities to work directly with individual students or small groups?
- What opportunities do I provide for students to express their feelings and concerns?
- What role do I play in facilitating connections between students and other supportive adults?

Cultivating a strong classroom culture that prioritizes human connection and relationship building isn't something we can do in the first two weeks of the semester and then forget about the rest of the school year. Nurturing and maintaining relationships in the classroom is something we must prioritize and dedicate time to all year. Teachers can use the strategies in table 8.4 to work toward this goal.

Table 8.4: Strategies to Develop Strong Relationships with and among Students

Strategies to Develop Strong Relationships with and among Students	
Conversation Starters	Begin each class or group task with a quick informal conversation or icebreaker to encourage students to connect before jumping into an academic task. These quick chats are an opportunity for students to share something fun about themselves and build their relationships with one another so they are more likely to engage in academic conversation or collaboration. Examples: • Would you rather spend the day at the beach or in the snow? • If you could travel anywhere, where would you go and why? • If you could only eat one type of food for the rest of your life, what would it be? • What song is your go-to track right now?
Regular Check-ins Using a High/Low Format	Schedule regular one-on-one check-ins with students to discuss their academic progress and any personal concerns. Using a high/low structure encourages students to discuss something that is going really well and something they are struggling with or need to troubleshoot. Making time for these quick conversations as the class is self-pacing through a lesson shows that you care about them and their academic success.

Four-Corner Debate	The four-corner debate is an effective strategy to help students explore and appreciate a range of perspectives within the classroom.
	In this activity, each classroom corner is designated for a specific response: 1) strongly agree, 2) agree, 3) disagree, and 4) strongly disagree. The teacher presents various statements on diverse topics. Once students are grouped according to their perspectives, the teacher facilitates a discussion, inviting representatives from each corner to articulate their reasons.
	This strategy encourages an open exchange of ideas and helps students understand how different factors, such as cultural background, personal experiences, and societal influences, shape diverse viewpoints. The primary aims of this exercise are to foster a deeper understanding of and respect for varied opinions and to enhance students' critical thinking and debate skills.

AI Integration

The goal of incorporating AI at this final stage of the design process is to seamlessly integrate instructional strategies that strive to cultivate more resilient students. Teachers must help students develop the qualities of self-awareness, perseverance, adaptability, and strong relationships in every lesson. The opportunities students have to practice and hone these skills cannot come in the form of stand-alone lessons separate from the subject and grade-level curriculum. Instead, they must be woven into the fabric of our lessons. This ensures that fostering resilience (with its core elements of self-awareness, perseverance, adaptability, and strong relationships) complements and enhances the students' ability to learn key concepts and skills central to each lesson.

But as teachers read through our suggestions, they may feel like this is one more thing to add to their overflowing plates. No, no, no.

We would never add to your already daunting workload! And we don't want the goal of cultivating resilient learners to be an add-on or disconnected from the curriculum and learning objectives in your class. This is where AI comes in to save the day.

Leveraging AI as a thought partner at this stage in your design work significantly reduces the mental strain and time required to imagine how a specific strategy might be used in creative ways in the context of a lesson. Let's explore some scenarios.

Building Self-Awareness and Character Awareness into an English Lesson

A sixth-grade English teacher might ask, "How can I use mood check-ins to enhance my students' understanding of emotional themes in the short story 'Eleven' by Sandra Cisneros?"

In response, ChatGPT could provide a detailed, step-by-step explanation of how to integrate this technique into a lesson focused on identifying themes and how they develop in the short story. Here is a brief overview of the suggestions generated by AI:

1. Onboard students to the purpose and process of completing a mood meter check-in.
2. Ask students to complete the mood meter, reflecting on their current mood and what might be impacting it today.
3. As students read "Eleven," encourage them to pay close attention to Rachel's emotions and experiences.
4. After the reading, conduct another mood check-in. Ask students to reflect on whether their emotions shifted during the reading and why.
5. Facilitate a discussion or have students write a short reflection on how understanding their emotions helps them understand Rachel's emotional journey.

Another English teacher might ask students to assess the moods of multiple main characters in a text, identifying factors contributing to their moods with words and drawings. Then, students could compare those to their own mood meter and write a short compare-and-contrast paragraph or creating a Venn diagram with drawings. The possibilities are endless when bouncing ideas off AI!

Enhancing Sportsmanship and Safety in PE through Role-Play and Mindfulness

A seventh-grade physical education teacher covering a range of topics, like sportsmanship, teamwork, and safety, can leverage the STOP strategy, paired with role-play, to encourage students to practice mindfulness in a variety of scenarios they will likely find themselves in.

Keyword Alert!

The STOP strategy: A practical approach to managing stress and emotions by encouraging students to pause and reflect before reacting. The acronym stands for stop, take a breath, observe, and proceed. It helps learners respond to challenges more effectively and maintain emotional regulation.

That seventh-grade physical education teacher could ask, "My class is learning the basics of basketball and one standard reads, 'Students to demonstrate and utilize knowledge of psychological and sociological concepts, principles, and strategies that apply to the learning and performance of physical activity.' How can I use role-play paired with the STOP strategy to help students engage with psychological and sociological concepts, principles, and strategies?"

Here is an overview of ChatGPT's suggestion:

- Identify the specific psychological and sociological concepts you want to address. For basketball, this might include concepts like teamwork, communication, pressure handling, conflict resolution, and motivation.
- Create scenarios that occur in basketball games, like responding to aggressive behavior from an opponent or managing frustration after a personal mistake.
- Teach students the STOP strategy as a method to handle these situations mindfully.
- Assign groups a scenario and let them practice then act them out using STOP.
- Facilitate a discussion or reflective activity after each role-play.

As students get comfortable using this strategy to think about responding mindfully when emotions on a field or court run high, teachers can introduce new challenges. They can invite students to develop their own scenarios and allow small groups to engage in their own follow-up discussions. This approach gradually releases control to the learners.

Perseverance and Math Problems with Hook the Group

A high school geometry teacher who wants to infuse more creative problem-solving into a small-group, teacher-led instructional session on finding the area of a polygon can ask ChatGPT, "How can I pique student interest and engage my group in a collaborative problem-solving activity before I provide instruction on how to find the area of a polygon? The goal is to help them develop perseverance in approaching new and unfamiliar math problems and utilize prior knowledge creatively."

ChatGPT suggests the following. We've trimmed it down, but you get the gist!

- Present students with an image of a polygon on a graph, preferably one that can be broken down into simpler shapes.
- Strategically pair students and ask them to apply various geometric formulas and strategies to try to find the area of the polygon.
- Listen to their conversations and note the strong strategies used and the misconceptions.
- Facilitate a short debrief of how they attempted to solve this unfamiliar problem.
- Provide differentiated instruction, using what you observed to target the specific needs of this group.

Regular problem-solving sessions with classmates do more than just boost students' skills in tackling new and tough math problems; they also build perseverance. Students see how teamwork can help them push past challenges that might seem too hard to handle alone.

These sessions also help students to see their classmates as valuable resources. This creates a supportive atmosphere where learners are encouraged to take risks and keep trying, knowing their peers have their back.

Developing Adaptability through Gold Rush Scenarios

A fifth-grade history teacher can integrate scenario-based learning into a unit focused on California history by asking ChatGPT, "How can I use scenario-based learning in my lessons on the gold rush to deepen my students' understanding of the historical context, challenges, and implications of events in American history?"

Below is the condensed version of ChatGPT's suggestions about how to integrate this strategy:

- Begin by introducing the gold rush so students understand the origins, key events, significant figures, and socioeconomic impacts, etc.
- Assign students roles (e.g., prospector, mining company owner, shopkeeper selling supplies, local sheriff).
- Give each group a scenario like the one pictured in table 8.5. It should require them to make decisions and solve relevant problems.
- Provide time for groups to engage in discussion and negotiation as well as reference resources while they work through their scenario to reach a specific outcome.

Table 8.5: Gold Rush Scenario-Based Learning Example (Thanks, ChatGPT!)

The Scenario: The Claim Dispute	
Background	You are a prospector who has been mining in a region of California known for rich gold deposits. After weeks of hard work, you've finally struck gold in a section of the riverbank. However, just as you begin to celebrate your find, another prospector arrives and claims that they have legal rights to this section of land. They show a claim deed that appears to be valid. The local sheriff is days away, and tensions are rising as more gold is uncovered.
Objective	Resolve the claim dispute in a manner that maximizes your gold yield, maintains peaceful relations, and respects legal boundaries.

Challenges	1. Validation of claim: You need to determine the authenticity of the opposing prospector's claim deed. This may involve consulting with other miners or local experts who can verify the signatures or dates on the deed. 2. Negotiation: If the claim is valid, you must negotiate with the other prospector to find a mutually beneficial agreement. Options might include sharing the mining rights, buying them out, or trading part of your own claimed land. 3. Alternative mining strategies: Prepare for the possibility that you might lose access to the current spot. Investigate other potential mining areas you can move to quickly, or consider different mining techniques that might yield gold more efficiently elsewhere. 4. Community relations: Handle the situation in a way that maintains or enhances your reputation among other miners and locals. This could affect your future business dealings and partnerships in the community. 5. Preparation for legal actions: Gather evidence and prepare arguments for a legal dispute, in case the matter escalates once the sheriff arrives.
Task for Students	• Work in groups to come up with a strategy that addresses all the above challenges. Each group must present their resolution strategy, outlining how they will validate the claim, negotiate with the other prospector, explore alternative mining options, manage their reputation in the community, and prepare for potential legal proceedings. • After presenting, students will receive feedback from the class and discuss what could be the best overall strategy considering the circumstances.

Scenario-based learning encourages students to think critically and adapt to a complex situation, developing key skills in negotiation, legal reasoning, and strategic planning. It also helps students get to know one another and build relationships as they navigate complex collaborative tasks.

Using Four-Corner Debate to Deepen a Science Lesson and Build Class Community

Imagine a science teacher wants to engage a fifth-grade class in a review of their unit on space systems, specifically the stars and the solar system. They might ask, "I'm teaching fifth-grade science using NGSS science standards, and I want to use four-corner debates to get kids discussing what they learned in our Space Systems: Stars and the Solar System unit. What prompts might I use during this debate to get them reviewing key concepts and ideas?"

ChatGPT generates a collection of prompts teachers can use to facilitate this debate, asking students if they strongly agree, agree, strongly disagree, or disagree. Here are examples:

- The Sun is the most important part of our solar system.
- The Moon has more influence on Earth than the Sun.
- Planets closer to the Sun are more likely to support life than those further away.

Once students have taken their position in the corner of the room that aligns with their opinion, the teacher can invite each corner to have a quick chat about their reasoning. After small-group huddles and chats, teachers can ask students from each corner to share their perspective.

Using the four-corner debate in your space systems unit not only deepens understanding of specific science concepts, but it also fosters relationship building. By sharing their diverse perspectives on planetary life or the role of gravity, students enhance their communication skills and empathy, learning to appreciate different viewpoints. This active engagement fosters effective collaboration and respect, cultivating a supportive environment where students feel connected and valued as they explore complex scientific concepts.

Ultimately, the final stage of our AI-enhanced design framework focuses on helping students cultivate skills critical to navigating dynamic and challenging learning environments. By leveraging AI to integrate these resilience-building strategies into lessons and learning activities, we can nurture confident, flexible, and strategic learners while also deepening their understanding of key concepts and skills. This focus on the qualities at the core of resilience is not to simply prepare students for the immediate challenges of school; it also sets them up for long-term success beyond the classroom. By focusing on developing these essential skills, we ensure that our students are not only academically proficient but also prepared to tackle whatever the future holds!

From Design Pathway to Learning Pathway

If you take our AI-enhanced design framework and invert it, as pictured in figure 8.2, you'll see that it depicts the learning pathway from a student's perspective. The first and most important step for a learner is developing the qualities necessary for resilience so they can navigate challenges and setbacks with confidence. The more time and effort students spend developing the skills at the heart of resilience—self-awareness, perseverance, adaptability, and strong relationships and social support—the more likely they are to successfully traverse the learning pathway to achieve the desired results.

Figure 8.2: The Learning Pathway

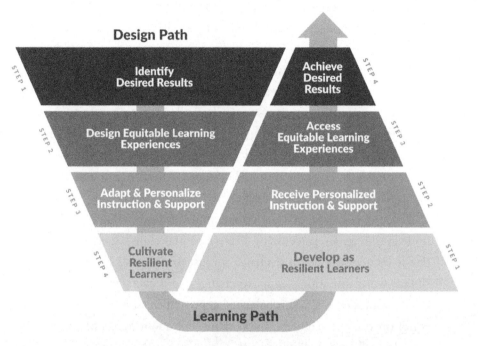

As students develop self-awareness and perseverance, their ability to advocate for their specific needs within the learning environment also improves. They will gain a clearer understanding of their strengths, limitations, and needs, making it easier for them to seek personalized support and instruction when grappling with complex concepts or challenging tasks. A self-aware student is more likely to admit confusion and seek help. For educators, this proactive communication simplifies our work, allowing us to tailor our efforts based on students' expressed needs rather than rely solely on data to gauge their progress toward individual learning objectives and the larger desired results of a unit.

Self-awareness and adaptability are crucial as students engage in universally designed blended learning experiences that emphasize student agency and offer meaningful choices, granting them greater control over their learning. Positioned as active participants, students face more cognitively and socially demanding situations than in traditional teacher-led, teacher-paced settings. This autonomy requires them to be self-motivated, resourceful, and strategic. Moreover, since learning is inherently a social endeavor, strong relationships with peers and teachers become essential, providing the necessary support for students to tackle challenging tasks effectively.

The irony of focusing on the content without an equal focus on nurturing the qualities necessary to thrive as a learner is that it can limit the depth and retention of learning. Without the foundation of resilience, students may struggle to apply knowledge in new or challenging contexts, missing opportunities for growth and deeper understanding. By prioritizing these essential skills *alongside* academic content, we equip students not just to pass tests but to excel in real-world situations, adapt to changes, and overcome obstacles throughout their lives. This balanced approach ensures that learning is not only about acquiring information but about becoming more capable, well-rounded individuals.

One-Sentence Summary

When teachers plan using the comprehensive design framework discussed in this book, they foster resilience in students by equipping them with the essential skills of self-awareness, perseverance, adaptability, and relationship building, empowering them to navigate both academic and real-world challenges with confidence.

Reflect and Discuss

1. How do you currently support the development of resilience in your students? Are there specific strategies or activities you use that have been particularly effective?

2. Considering the qualities of resilient learners discussed in this chapter (self-awareness, perseverance, adaptability, strong

relationships), which do you think is most challenging to develop in your students? Why?

3. How can AI-enhanced resilience-building strategies be integrated into your existing curriculum? Are there particular topics, subjects, or skills where this integration could be most beneficial?

4. Discuss how cultivating resilience in students might change the way you approach teaching and classroom management. What shifts in your teaching practice might be necessary?

5. How does the concept of resilience intersect with other educational goals, like inclusivity, accessibility, equity, and student-led learning?

Time to Apply!

Let's take what you learned in this chapter about cultivating resilient learners and put it into practice with a little help from AI.

- **Step 1:** Select a quality central to resilience that you want to focus on for this application activity—self-awareness, perseverance, adaptability, or strong relationships and social support.
- **Step 2:** Choose a lesson to focus on for this exercise and revisit the learning objective for it. Then, imagine you are going to add a second learning objective focused on developing the quality you selected in step 1. To craft your learning objective, fill in the statement below:

    Students will develop [quality] by [insert learning task].
- **Step 3:** Select a strategy presented in this chapter (or one you generate using AI) to integrate into this lesson that will help students develop the quality you selected in step 1. Remember, you want this strategy to be an opportunity to develop a quality key to resilience while also deepening

students' understanding of content area concepts or skills in the lesson.

- **Step 4:** Give your revised lesson to a colleague to review and provide feedback!

CONCLUSION

The Quirks of
Humanizing ChatGPT

Katie Sometimes, when I work with ChatGPT, I talk to it like it's my assistant—and I have serious issues with empathy. I get frustrated and resort to ALL CAPS exclamations like "STOP mentioning learning styles. THEY don't exist." It's like it knows how to push my buttons! My neck gets itchy, my pulse quickens, and then I think, *Goodness gracious, you're arguing with a robot. Settle down.*

I've created a persona of a haggard ChatGPT assistant, and this person is expected to know exactly what I'm thinking and refill my coffee while they're at it (oh, that would be amazing!). I'm basically the boss from *The Devil Wear Prada* when I'm interacting with bots. Although ChatGPT makes my work much more efficient, it doesn't bring me joy like a real human would, and it drives me to frustration much more quickly. Certainly, I could co-author a book with ChatGPT, but it wouldn't be nearly as rewarding as writing a book with Cat.

Whenever Cat reaches out, which is usually at a ridiculously early hour and without a doubt while she is sipping coffee in bed, she shares an incredible idea for a book via text and gives me the option to dive in. My answer is always an emphatic "YES!" I love working with her because she is brilliant, creative, and one of the best teachers I have ever known—but also because she has become a dear friend, and I love her as a human. Quite simply, Cat and I have a connection that AI and I will never have.

The lack of deep relationships in education is evident everywhere, even in professional development settings. Sometimes, I present at a conference, and amazingly hardworking educators arrive to learn more about UDL and how to shift to student-led practices. But as I walk around, I see people are consumed with entering grades, checking emails, and using AI to be more productive, switching back and forth between tabs. Believe me, I've seen it all while giving a talk, and I dish out absolutely no judgment. I find myself doing the same things.

In some ways, artificial intelligence has the potential to make us more efficient and focused. However, it requires us to be purposeful so that we don't simply fill the space that technology has cleared with other tasks, continuing to spin around and around on the proverbial hamster wheel of educator prep. So, how can we better leverage technology to increase our efficacy while freeing us up to spend our time making vital human connections? Luckily, research paves the way.

Strong Pedagogical Practices

We get it. The work just keeps piling up, and it seems like we won't be able to dig our way out of it, so it begins to seep into our lives. As much as we tell ourselves we can multitask, the research is pretty clear that doing so is impossible. Multitasking is actually just a phenomenon called *task switching*, which is exactly what it sounds like. This involves a *switch cost*, which is the time and mental energy required to shift attention from one task to another. This constant shifting can significantly reduce productivity.

For example, research has shown that attempting to multitask can increase the time it takes to complete tasks by as much as 40 percent.[1] Each switch might waste only a fraction of a second, but that lost time adds up when people repeatedly switch back and forth between tasks. Moreover, a study published in the *Journal of Experimental Psychology: Human Perception and Performance* found that multitasking can also reduce productivity by up to 40 percent.[2] This continual juggling act doesn't just hinder efficiency; it also degrades the quality of our work and diminishes our capacity to forge meaningful human connections.

Often, when we are working with teachers, we begin with an optimistic opening speech that encourages attendees to think about what they need to do to stay focused and productive. Common strategies include turning off notifications, stowing away phones, and resisting the urge to multitask. While we may recognize that multitasking isn't effective, it's a habit many of us fall into anyway. However, the potential for meaningful connections and conversations at conferences highlights that the cost of task switching extends beyond productivity; it hinders the essential human connections that can be built among educators. And this has a significant impact.

Human connection in learning (especially for adult learners) facilitates collective understanding and increased efficacy.[3] For example, consider a group of teachers attending a professional development workshop. When they engage in collaborative activities, share experiences, and discuss strategies, they build a sense of camaraderie and trust. This is driven by social synchrony, which inherently helps us connect and empathize with others. Just as social synchrony allows individuals to align their actions and emotions for greater connection and understanding, it helps teachers align their strategies and collaborative efforts in educational settings. This enables teachers to work cohesively toward common goals, support each other's efforts, and believe in their collective capacity to positively impact student outcomes. Essentially, human connection strengthens the team aspect of teaching, making the group more effective than individuals working in isolation.

So, ironically, we want to end this book by leveraging AI's brilliance to remind us of strategies for centering our work's human elements. Our friend ChatGPT had some amazing ideas when we gave it the following prompt:

> Could you provide detailed strategies for balancing tasks that require personal interaction versus those that can be managed with AI? Please include tips on effectively scheduling these tasks throughout the day, suggest innovative meeting formats that minimize digital distractions, and offer guidance on dedicating specific times for engaging with colleagues to enhance workplace interpersonal connections.

Here are some of our favorite ideas for how ChatGPT thought we should, well, use ChatGPT:

- Every morning, create two lists: one for tasks that require human sensitivity and connection (e.g., counseling students, engaging in discussions with colleagues) and another for tasks that can be automated or assisted by AI (e.g., drafting lessons, creating rubrics, drafting reminder emails).

- Assign specific times in the day for AI-assisted tasks and strictly human tasks. This approach minimizes the need to switch back and forth, helping maintain focus and effectiveness in each type of task.

- Instead of traditional sit-down meetings, suggest standing meetings or walking meetings. This can stimulate more dynamic conversations away from the digital distractions of desks and devices.

> • Block off specific times on your calendar as "connection time" dedicated to engaging with colleagues. This could be for casual catch-ups, collaborative brainstorming sessions, or coffee breaks.

We love ChatGPT's suggestions here, but truly, we don't feel like we needed the robot for this advice. We all know that we need to take some time to disconnect from technology and connect with ourselves and each other—whether that's enjoying a cocktail or coffee with a dear friend, nurturing a hobby like knitting or running, or taking time to sit on a beach, take a hike, or pet our dogs. There is something beautiful about the world around us that simply cannot be replicated online. Throughout our careers and lives, we must make time to be present in the here and now, soak in the moment, and realize that there is a beautiful world around us. We want to use technology so we have more time to enjoy it, not less. And it is critical that we make time to completely disconnect, as the constant multitasking isn't good for us.

Juggling multiple tasks—like toggling between ChatGPT, email, and social media—can drain our cognitive resources, impair our focus, and negatively affect our mental health. To combat this, it's vital to establish clear priorities when you plan your day: as ChatGPT itself suggested, set aside specific times for different tasks, silence notifications, and focus on one thing at a time. Implement structured routines during your professional learning community meetings, prep periods, or even personal time, such as when you're watching TV in the evening. (Catlin and I shamelessly love *The Bachelor*!) After completing tasks, remember to reconnect with the world around you, perhaps by spending time with your pet (shout-out to our dogs, Lyla and Birdie) or calling a friend (remember when you used phones as phones?).

The adage "AI is not going to take your job; someone using AI will" underscores the importance of not just being busy but being productive—which requires us to slow down, establish routines, and focus on what truly matters. This holistic approach can transform how we integrate technology into our lives, ensuring that we use tools like AI to enhance, rather than complicate, our professional and personal time.

The moment when Catlin and I transitioned from colleagues to friends happened in Panama City, where we were co-presenting at a conference for the Tri-Association, a network of international schools across the Caribbean, South America, and Central America. Despite our overwhelming to-do lists and the barrage of emails, we decided to disconnect and take a moment for ourselves. We sipped mojitos on the beach, shared stories from our childhood (who would have guessed we both grew up with Samoyeds?), and planned the perfect morning together. The next day, our agenda included working out while listening to scandalous murder mysteries on our earbuds, grabbing coffees (minus dairy for Cat), and making memories (including a few TikTok videos which will never see the light of day!).

That trip marked the beginning of a friendship that we continue to nurture through Zoom calls, endless texts and voice memos, and the seeds we are planting for a real vacation! Our shared experiences and mutual support have enriched our work and made this book (and hopefully many others) possible. The human connection we established on that trip continues to inspire and motivate us, underscoring the importance of relationships in both our personal and professional lives.

One-Sentence Summary

Although AI can enhance productivity, we must not forget the importance of balance, mental health, and nurturing human relationships so we can show up as the best educators we can possibly be.

Reflect and Discuss

1. Reflect on a time when technology improved your productivity. Did this increase in efficiency allow you more time to engage in meaningful interactions, or did you find yourself filling the time with more tasks? How did this affect your stress levels and job satisfaction?

2. Discuss the concept of *switch cost*. How might understanding and managing this help you balance the use of AI in your professional life?

3. Considering the emphasis on social synchrony and collective efficacy, how can educators better design learning experiences that balance technological tools and the need for human interaction?

4. Explore the idea that "AI is not going to take your job; someone using AI will." What strategies can you employ to ensure you are using AI as a tool for enhancement and not disruption?

REFERENCES

Chapter 1

1 Claire R. Kilbane and Natalie B. Milman, *Teaching Models: Designing Instruction for 21st Century Learners* (Boston: Pearson, 2014), 3.

2 Andrea Prado Tuma et al., *What K–12 English Language Arts and Mathematics Instructional Materials Were Newly Purchased and Used for the 2021–2022 School Year? Findings from the 2022 American* (Santa Monica, CA: RAND Corporation, 2022), 2.

3 Prado Tuma, *What K–12*, [2] .

4 Kilbane and Milman, *Teaching Models*.

5 Jay McTighe and Peggy L. Brown, "Using Understanding by Design to Make the Standards Come Alive," *Science Scope* 45, no. 2 (2021): 28–33.

6 Grant Wiggins and Jay McTighe, *Understanding by Design*. (Alexandria, VA: Association for Supervision and Curriculum Development, 2005), 15.

7 Grant Wiggins and Jay McTighe, *The Understanding by Design Guide to Creating High-Quality Units* (Alexandria, VA: ASCD, 2011).

8 Collaborative for Academic, Social, and Emotional Learning (CASEL), "What Is the CASEL Framework?" last modified 2024, https://casel.org/fundamentals-of-sel/what-is-the-casel-framework.

9 Joseph A. Durlak, Joseph L. Mahoney, and Abigail E. Boyle, "What We Know, and What We Need to Find Out about Universal, School-Based Social and Emotional Learning Programs for Children and Adolescents: A Review of Meta-Analyses and Directions for Future Research," *Psychological Bulletin* 148, no. 11–12 (2022).

10 Christina Cipriano et al., *Stage 2 Report: The State of the Evidence for Social and Emotional Learning: A Contemporary Meta-Analysis of Universal School-Based SEL Interventions*, last modified February 3, 2023, https://osf.io/preprints/osf/mk35u.

11 Catlin R. Tucker and Katie Novak, *The Shift to Student-Led: Reimagining Classroom Workflows with UDL and Blended Learning* (Impress, 2022) .

12 Robert C. Pianta, "Teacher–Student Interactions: Measurement, Impacts, Improvement, and Policy," *Policy Insights from the Behavioral and Brain Sciences* 3, no. 1 (2016): 98–105.

13 Barbara Bray and Kathleen McClaskey, *Personalization vs. Differentiation vs. Individualization Report* (v3), 2018. https://kathleenmcclaskey.com/2018/01/24/personalization-vs-differentiation-vs-individualization-pdi-chart-v3-infographic/.

14 Digital Promise Global, *Learner Variability Is the Rule, Not the Exception*, by Barbara Pape, 2018, https://digitalpromise.org/wp-content/uploads/2018/06/Learner-Variability-Is-The-Rule.pdf.

Chapter 2

1   Ronald Heifetz and Donald L. Laurie, "The Work of Leadership," *Harvard Business Review* 79, no. 11 (2001): 131–141, https://hbr.org/2001/12/the-work-of-leadership.

2   Ayesha Akhlaq, "Translating Literature to Code." *Root and STEM* 7 (spring 2023): [48], https://pinnguaq.com/wp-content/uploads/2023/04/root-stem-spring-2023-digital-final.pdf.

3   The Danielson Group, "The Framework for Teaching," [September 20, 2024], https://danielsongroup.org/the-framework-for-teaching/.

4   Robert Kegan and Lisa Lahey, "The Real Reason People Won't Change," *Harvard Business Review* 79, no. 10 (November 2001): 85–92, https://hbr.org/2001/11/the-real-reason-people-wont-change.

Chapter 3

1   Education Week, "What's the Purpose of Standards in Education? An Explainer," by Sarah Schwartz, last modified July 2023, https://www.edweek.org/teaching-learning/whats-the-purpose-of-standards-in-education-an-explainer/2023/07.

2   Wiggins and McTighe, *Understanding by Design*.

3   Wiggins and McTighe, *Understanding by Design*.

4   Deborah Reed, "Clearly Communicating the Learning Objective Matters!" *Middle School Journal* 43, no. 3 (2012).

5   Barbara Osueke, Brook Mekonnen, and Jenny D. Stanton, "How Undergraduate Science Students Use Learning Objectives to Study," *Journal of Microbiology and Biology Education* 19, no. 2 (2018).

Chapter 4

1   Shelley Moore, "Learning Continuum Resources," accessed August 1, 2024, https://blogsomemoore.com/learning-continuum-resources/.

2   Erika A. Patall, Harris Cooper, and J. Civey Robinson, "The Effects of Choice on Intrinsic Motivation and Related Outcomes: A Meta-Analysis of Research Findings," *Psychological Bulletin* 134, no. 2 (2008): 270–300.

3   Catlin Tucker, *Balance with Blended Learning: Partner with Your Students to Reimagine Learning and Reclaim Your Life* (Thousand Oaks, CA: Corwin, 2020).

Chapter 5

1   Sharon Otterman, "New Library Is a $41.5 Million Masterpiece. But about Those Stairs," *The New York Times*, November 5, 2019, https://www.nytimes.com/2019/11/05/nyregion/long-island-city-library.html.

2   Mojtaba Badali et al., "The Role of Motivation in MOOCs' Retention Rates: A Systematic Literature Review," *Research and Practice in Technology Enhanced Learning* 17, no. 1 (2022): 1–20.

3   Veenita Shah, Sahana Murthy, and Sridhar Iyer. "Is My MOOC Learner-Centric? A Framework for Formative Evaluation of MOOC Pedagogy," *The International Review of Research in Open and Distributed Learning* 24, no. 2 (2023): 138–161.

4   Catlin Tucker, *The Complete Guide to Blended Learning* (Bloomington, IN: Solution Tree, 2022).

5   CAST, *UDL Guidelines*, accessed August 1, 2024, https://udlguidelines.cast.org/.

Chapter 6

1   Richard Ryan and Edward Deci, *Self-Determination Theory: Basic Psychological Needs in Motivation, Development, and Wellness* (New York: Guilford Press, 2018).

2   Ryan and Deci, *Self-Determination Theory*.

3   John Marshall Reeve, "Why Teachers Adopt a Controlling Motivating Style toward Students and How They Can Become More Autonomy Supportive," *Educational Psychologist* 44, no. 3 (2009): 159–175.

4   Chia Jung Wang, et al., "Competence, Autonomy, and Relatedness in the Classroom: Understanding Students' Motivational Processes Using the Self-Determination Theory," *Heliyon* 5, no. 7 (2019).

5   Developing the Skill of Learning with James Anderson," January 30, 2024, hosted by Catlin Tucker, *On the Balance*, podcast audio, [time stamp if relevant], https://catlinthebalance.podbean.com/e/elevating-learning-from-an-act-to-an-art-with-james-anderson/.

6   Marzano Resources, "Tips from Dr. Marzano: The Highly Engaged Classroom," last modified 2024, https://www.marzanoresources.com/resources/tips/hec_tips_archive.

Chapter 7

1   University of Virginia School of Education and Human Development, "Renowned Educator and Scholar Carol Tomlinson Defined a New Way of Teaching," by Audrey Breen, October 9, 2019, https://education.virginia.edu/news-stories/renowned-educator-and-scholar-carol-tomlinson-defined-new-way-teaching.

2   Melissa Brink and David E. Bartz, "Effective Use of Formative Assessment by High School Teachers," *Practical Assessment, Research, and Evaluation* 22, no. 1 (2017).

3   Katie McGlynn and Jennifer Kelly, "Using Formative Assessments to Differentiate Instruction," *Science Scope* 41, no. 2 (2017): 22–25.

Chapter 8

1   Emmy E. Werner, "Resilience Research: Past, Present, and Future," in *Resilience in Children, Families, and Communities: Linking Context to Practice and Policy*, edited by Ray D. Peters, Bonnie Leadbeater, and Robert J. McMahon (Boston: Springer US, 2005), 3–11.

2   Maddy Reinert, Deborah Fritze, and Theresa Nguyen. *The State of Mental Health in America 2022* (Alexandria, VA: Mental Health America, 2021), 25.

3   Syed Rahman et al., "The Development of Expert Learners in the Classroom," *Contemporary Issues in Education Research* 3, no. 6 (2010): 1–8.

4   National Scientific Council on the Developing Child. Supportive Relationships and Active Skill-Building Strengthen the Foundations of Resilience: Working Paper 13. http://www.developingchild.harvard.edu (2015): 1.

5   Karen Reivich and Andrew Shatté, *The Resilience Factor: 7 Keys to Finding Your Inner Strength and Overcoming Life's Hurdles* (New York: Three Rivers Press, 2003), 3–4.

6   Julia Moeller et al., "High School Students' Feelings: Discoveries from a Large National Survey and an Experience Sampling Study," *Learning and Instruction* 66 (April 2020).

7   Angela Duckworth, *Grit: The Power of Passion and Perseverance* (New York: Scribner, 2016).

8   Carol S. Dweck, *Mindset: The New Psychology of Success* (New York: Random House, 2006).

9   Andrew J. Martin et al., "Adaptability: Conceptual and Empirical Perspectives on Responses to Change, Novelty, and Uncertainty," *Australian Journal of Guidance and Counselling* 22, no. 1 (2012): 58–81.

10 Martin et al., "Adaptability."

11 Emmy E. Werner. "Resilience Research: Past, Present, and Future." In *Resilience in Children, Families, and Communities: Linking Context to Practice and Policy*, ed. Ray D. Peters, Bonnie Leadbeater, and Robert J. McMahon, 3–11. Boston: Springer US, 2005.

12 Emmy E. Werner. "Resilience in Development." *Current Directions in Psychological Science* 4, no. 3 (1995): 81–85.

13 Ronald D. Taylor and Azeb Gebre, "Teacher–Student Relationships and Personalized Learning: Implications of Person and Contextual Variables," in *Handbook on Personalized Learning for States, Districts, and Schools*, edited by Marilyn Murphy, Sam Redding, and Janet S. Twyman (Philadelphia, PA: Center on Innovations in Learning, Temple University, 2016), 205.

Conclusion

1   American Psychological Association, "Multitasking," [access date], https://www.apa.org/topics/research/multitasking.

2   Joshua Rubinstein, David E. Meyer, and Jeffrey E. Evans, "Executive Control of Cognitive Processes in Task Switching," *PsycEXTRA Dataset*, 1994.

3   Stephanie MacMahon, "Human Connection and Learning," *ACCESS: Contemporary Issues in Education* 40, no. 1 (September 1, 2020): 15–23. https://doi.org/10.46786/ac20.9176.

Acknowledgments

From Catlin: Katie, you're my go-to for everything—from fashion tips to navigating trolls on X and always knowing the best murder mystery to dive into! Whether we're chatting about travel must-dos before work trips, rocking fun looks from Rent the Runway, or sharing our love of heels, coffee, dogs, and family, I always feel lucky to have you in my corner. Your energy, expertise, and generosity are a gift to me and all the educators who have the privilege of working with you! I feel lucky to call you a friend!

Jay McTighe, your work with Grant Wiggins has profoundly shaped my approach to educational design and the way I approached this book. I am incredibly grateful that our paths crossed at the AISA Conference all those years ago. Your dedication to improving education resonates deeply with me, and I always look forward to your emails, knowing they'll offer valuable insights or a clever remark that brings a smile. I truly appreciate the lasting impact your work has had on me personally and on the broader educational community. Thank you for continuing to inspire and challenge us all.

Cheyenne and Maddox, I love you more than life itself. I know most parents do not enjoy the teenage years, but this is my favorite age. I love watching you grow into young adults with your own passions, relationships, and dreams for the future. You challenge me constantly to be a better parent and person, and for that, I'm so grateful. I am so proud to be your mom and cannot wait to see what you do as you go out into the world. No matter where you go or what you do, I will be there to love, support, and celebrate you!

Christopher, you've brought so much love and joy into my life. I love our long hikes with Lyla, slow mornings with coffee, end-of-the-day chats on the porch, and HQ collaborations! Whether we're being silly and cracking up or tackling a project together, I love that we can balance both. Thank you for sharing your incredible creative talents and always encouraging me to think bigger. You continue to inspire me—in my work and in life—and I'm so grateful for you, love.

Hey, little Harper! Welcome to this world. You are a little ray of sunshine, making life that much more beautiful. You and Cash are a constant source of joy for me. Being your Auntie is the best. I love you very much!

Thank you to George and Paige for continuing to believe in our work and welcoming our collaborations! We appreciate you making our work available to educators everywhere!

Katie: Catlin, I feel so damn blessed that we found each other in this big, beautiful world. Truly, and I know we both say this a lot, but you are one of my favorite humans. I love our collaborative projects and how you push me to be a better educator and writer. I always learn so much from our conversations and can't even put into words how much I love our virtual two-person murder mystery book club. I'm definitely holding you to that couples writing retreat to celebrate our next fabulous project. I'll just wait for your 5 a.m. text with a new idea, and from there, the universe will take it where it will! You say jump, girlfriend, and I'll always say, "How high?"

David Rose, when you called me the other day, I felt like I was getting a phone call from an A-list celebrity (wait, I was, wasn't I?!). Your work on UDL and constant mentorship are a huge reason I am where I am today. As I review my work, I always try to view it through the lens of the groundbreaking work you did in what my kids would call "The 1900s." Truly, you were one of the first to call out the significant inequities in one-size-fits-all education, and I hope my work aligns with the incredible work you started. Can't wait for coffee soon! Xoxo

Nani, Bapa, Lindie, and Jerms, goodness gracious, did I hit the jackpot with you? Many of my best stories and analogies come from all the amazing adventures we've had over the past forty-five years, and I'm sure there are so many more to come. #thibnuclear and #sibbies for the win!

Lon, Torin, Aylin, Brec, Boden, and Birdie (aka Pigsley, Chunky Sparkle, and Bird Brain), this whole book is about the fact that robots are pretty rad and amazing, but the heart of teaching and learning will always be human. I think that's a pretty good rule for relationships as well. Connecting with friends via Snapchat, text, Fortnite, and Roblox chat is cool, but never ever stop hitting the Sandlot, staying up past your bedtimes at the firepit, and making real memories (well, maybe not the ones that involve covering each other in condiments). Love you all more than you will ever know.

George and Paige, thank you for continuing to take a chance on these two wild sisters you never knew you needed in your life!

About the Authors

About **Dr. Catlin Tucker** is a bestselling author, international trainer, and keynote speaker. She was named Teacher of the Year in 2010 in Sonoma County, where she taught for 16 years. Catlin earned her BA in English literature from the University of California at Los Angeles. She earned her English credential and master's in Education at the University of California at Santa  Barbara. In 2020, Catlin earned her doctorate in learning technologies at Pepperdine University.

Catlin designs and facilitates professional learning experiences that empower leaders and teachers to cultivate the mindset, skill set, and tool set needed to design equitable, student-centered learning environments. She focuses on data-informed design, differentiation, and personalized learning to meet the diverse needs of all students. By leveraging technology strategically, Catlin helps educators transition from being the sole source of expertise to facilitators who actively engage students as agents in their own learning. She also collaborates with leadership teams and instructional coaches to create professional learning infrastructures that embed growth and innovation into the fabric of the school community, ensuring sustainable and meaningful change.

Catlin has written a series of bestselling books, including *The Shift to Student-led*, *The Complete Guide to Blended Learning*, *UDL and Blended Learning*, and *Balance with Blended Learning*. She hosts *The Balance* podcast and is active on X @Catlin_Tucker and Instagram @CatlinTucker. You can learn about Catlin's work on her website, CatlinTucker.com.

About Katie Novak

Katie Novak, Ed.D., is an internationally renowned education consultant, author, graduate instructor at the University of Pennsylvania, and a former assistant superintendent of schools in Massachusetts. With over twenty years of experience in teaching and administration, an earned doctorate in curriculum and teaching, and sixteen published books, Katie designs and presents workshops both nationally and internationally, focusing on the implementation of inclusive practices, Universal Design for Learning (UDL), multi-tiered systems of support, and universally designed leadership. Novak's work has impacted educators worldwide, as her contributions and collaborations have built upon the foundation for an educational framework that is critical for student success.

Dr. Novak is the author of the best-selling books *UDL Now!: A Teacher's Guide to Applying Universal Design for Learning in Today's Classrooms*, *Innovate Inside the Box*, with George Couros, *Equity by*

Design, with Mirko Chardin, and *UDL and Blended Learning* and *The Shift to Student-Led* with Catlin Tucker.

Novak's work has been highlighted in many publications including *Edutopia*, *Cult of Pedagogy*, *Language*, *The Inclusion Lab* magazine, *NAESP Principal*, *ADDitude* magazine, *Commonwealth* magazine, the Huffington Post, *Principal Leadership*, *District Administrator*, *ASCD Education Update*, and *School Administrator*. You can learn more about Katie at novakeducation.com. She is also active on social media at @KatieNovakUDL.

More from

IMPRESS

ImpressBooks.org

Empower: What Happens When Students Own Their Learning by A.J. Juliani and John Spencer

Learner-Centered Innovation: Spark Curiosity, Ignite Passion, and Unleash Genius by Katie Martin

Unleash Talent: Bringing Out the Best in Yourself and the Learners You Serve by Kara Knollmeyer

Reclaiming Our Calling: Hold On to the Heart, Mind, and Hope of Education by Brad Gustafson

Take the L.E.A.P.: Ignite a Culture of Innovation by Elisabeth Bostwick

Drawn to Teach: An Illustrated Guide to Transforming Your Teaching written by Josh Stumpenhorst and illustrated by Trevor Guthke

Math Recess: Playful Learning in an Age of Disruption by Sunil Singh and Dr. Christopher Brownell

Innovate inside the Box: Empowering Learners Through UDL and Innovator's Mindset by George Couros and Katie Novak

Personal & Authentic: Designing Learning Experiences That Last a Lifetime by Thomas C. Murray

Learner-Centered Leadership: A Blueprint for Transformational Change in Learning Communities by Devin Vodicka

Kids These Days: A Game Plan for (Re)Connecting with Those We Teach, Lead, & Love by Dr. Jody Carrington

UDL and Blended Learning: Thriving in Flexible Learning Landscapes by Katie Novak and Catlin Tucker

Teachers These Days: Stories & Strategies for Reconnection by Dr. Jody Carrington and Laurie McIntosh

Because of a Teacher: Stories of the Past to Inspire the Future of Education written and curated by George Couros

Because of a Teacher, Volume 2: Stories from the First Years of Teaching written and curated by George Couros

Evolving Education: Shifting to a Learner-Centered Paradigm by Katie Martin

Adaptable: How to Create an Adaptable Curriculum and Flexible Learning Experiences That Work in Any Environment by A.J. Juliani

Lead from Where You Are: Building Intention, Connection, and Direction in Our Schools by Joe Sanfelippo

The Shift to Student-Led: Reimagining Classroom Workflows with UDL and Blended Learning by Catlin R. Tucker & Katie Novak

The Design Thinking Classroom: Using Design Thinking to Reimagine the Role and Practice of Educators by David Jakes

Shift Writing into the Classroom with UDL and Blended Learning by Catlin R. Tucker and Katie Novak

Teach Happy: Small Steps to Big Joy by Kim Strobel

What Makes a Great Principal by George Couros and Allyson Apsey

Made in the USA
Las Vegas, NV
15 January 2025

16450000R00138